THE CORPORATE CHRISTIAN

BOOK 3

The Hidden War

PASTOR OWEN E. WILLIAMS

First edition published 2019.
Second edition published 2023.

Cover Design: 99 Design by Vista
Author Photo: T. L. Holmes
Typesetting: Edge of Water Designs, edgeofwater.com

ISBNs:
   979-8-9874758-8-1 (Paperback)
   979-8-9874758-9-8 (eBook)

Publisher: Grapevine Publishing Press

DEDICATION

Thank you to my life partner and wife of thirty-three years, Elder Debora Williams. Thank you for your love, support, and daily prayers over my life. Thank you for your invaluable contribution to this trilogy; it could not be done without your continued support.

Elder Debora is an ordained minister of the Gospel of Jesus Christ, healthcare administrator, counselor, and church leader who has been a bright guiding light in my life and in the life of all those who she touches.

To my precious daughter, Desiree Rose Williams, who, in the last three years, has grown up and matured into such a beautiful and responsible young lady.

To the memories of my mother and father: I think about you every day and miss you dearly.

ENDORSEMENT

Deon Govender

I have known Pastor Owen Williams since the late 2000s when we met at a church meeting in Johannesburg. After several subsequent interactions (also at church meetings) in Johannesburg and New York, we developed a friendship. About seven years ago, Pastor Owen and I started collaborating on the rollout of a pastoral care training program he designed for nonprofit and community organizations in South Africa.

Through my walk with Pastor Owen, I have realized that he is passionate about healing people spiritually and psychologically by assisting them to liberate their minds from the trauma of past events. I have also realized that he truly lives at the crossroads where Christian life meets the corporate world. This, in my view, qualifies him to pen with authority the *Corporate Christian* book trilogy. But beyond living at these crossroads,

Pastor Owen is able to function (and counsel others to function) optimally at these intersections. His work experiences, ministry, and gifting have equipped him to relate to and empathize with the corporate Christian overwhelmed by workplace challenges. He draws on the Word of God and wisdom of Holy Spirit to offer insights and practical advice to such challenges.

This book, *The Corporate Christian III: The Hidden War* is for every Christian desiring fulfillment in the workplace, while being truly representative of the God he serves in that environment. It highlights how the Christian in the corporate workplace can easily be blocked from achieving such fulfillment if he cannot identify and respond appropriately to the hidden war at play.

The book will challenge the corporate Christian by pointing out the contradictions between spoken Christian values and the Christian's lived values in the workplace. It will highlight how this contradiction erodes our power to serve as change agents and influencers in our world. But it will also direct you as to how to walk in faith, live in love, and be victorious in battle. I trust that you will grow through this book.

Deon Govender is a corporate lawyer and corporate Christian. He practices as a cross-border finance lawyer out of an international law firm headquartered in Washington, DC. He lives in Johannesburg, South Africa, with his wife of twenty-three years, Rozetta, and his three daughters.

TABLE OF CONTENTS

PREFACE

This book is the last leg of a trilogy highlighting the complex dynamics between Christian faith and Christian love in the provoking, tempestuous, and enticing environments of the corporate world. It continues to be motivated by a real desire to serve and encourage members of the body of Christ who struggle to reconcile these two opposing dynamics in their daily lives, whether it be on the job, in their homes, their relationships, and even in their churches. This reconciliation can be challenging to believers. Its goal is to edify the believer on how to manage his/her behavior righteously, morally, and ethically in all environments. Another goal is to learn to assess ourselves and identify caution flags in our paths that block spiritual and emotional growth, while provoking and drawing out old natures and rebellious behavior that can so easily ensnare us into destructive expressions.

This book will also teach us how to trust and comply with God's universal word, the *logos*, while we apply the personal *rhema* word to daily living. We will learn how to walk in faith, live in love, and be victorious in battle, for if these three tenants are working in harmony, we are now living the well-balanced life that the apostle John spoke about in the third epistle of John: "Beloved, I pray that you may prosper in all things and be in health, just as your soul prospers" and your physical and spiritual states would be in excellent condition as well as in harmony with one another.

ACKNOWLEDGMENTS

I would like to take the opportunity to thank the following people, for without their contributors, this book would not be possible.

To my Lord and Savior Jesus Christ, who kept me in my right mind through it all, has looked past all of my sins and faults, and continues to pour out His divine will in my life.

To my beloved wife and life partner for the last twenty-nine years, for her continued love, support, and encouragement.

To my daughter: you continue to make me the proudest dad this side of heaven.

To my mother, who has gone home to be with the Lord: thank you for all of your trials and struggles in keeping the family together.

To the St. Mark Missionary Baptist Church: there is no finer place or greater people that I would rather serve God with than you. God bless you, and I love each and every one of you.

To Aunt Myrtle English for her endless love, compassion, and support in making these last two projects a reality.

The professors and support staff at Liberty University Baptist Theological Seminary: yours is a mixture of grace, love, and knowledge. God bless this great institution.

INTRODUCTION

Inside of every human being are two natures led by two distinct doctrines: theological and psychological. The theological doctrine is divine-focused while the psychological is self-focused. The ongoing battle for dominance within us is classified as spiritual war, but I have decided for this project to describe more narrowly and accurately as "hidden war." It's a daily ongoing war that affects every aspect of human existence. The ability to perceive, without bias, who we choose to have relationships with—whether they be social, professional, spiritual, commercial, or intimate—this battle will, in some way, affect the outcome. The following chapters will discuss in-depth the dynamics of our own personal battles, but as the front cover demonstrates, most people are nearly always unaware of both the Goliath in front of them and the David inside of them and that they are already fully equipped to run this race and overcome this world.

The complexities of this hidden war are what we call spiritual warfare with the intent on altering cognitive abilities and behavior. On this battlefield, victory will not come by way of carnal weapons, medications, or antidotes. The battle will attempt to stymie spiritual growth through faith by keeping us complacent in our circumstance and fearful of venturing outside of our comfort zones.[1] We tend to be conservative and cautious with how we are perceived while being extremely liberal with our perception of others, including God. This psychology is a self-first doctrine that produces an overabundance of individualism and "my way Christianity." The American society has allowed itself to be built on a falsehood of the past, the notion of the rugged American Western frontier. This Hollywood perspective of our past has been devoid of real human relationships between all people, where every man needed his neighbor to survive the elements, drought,

---

1   Jerry Falwell, *Building Dynamic Faith* (Nashville: Thomas Nelson, Inc. 2005), 73.

famine, and violence. Yet, what has been allowed to develop is an "every man for himself" doctrine.

So here we are, in this present day, as self-centered, arrogant, and prideful people who are continually at war within ourselves because of these theological versus psychological doctrines. This false past, its attitudes, and way of living has been compounded and promoted all over the land with the explosion of social media. No part of our society has been spared. We are prideful in our careers, our social lives, our churches, our finances, and even in child rearing. Aggressive and offensive attitudes of boastfulness, prideful, and arrogant speech and behavior confront us.

Beloved, in these environments, it becomes difficult to yield and or acquiesce to one another in a subservient manner. It will be my attempt to keep this topic the main focus of this book while we explore and journey through the vast wilderness of the human psyche and see how faith and love battle within this war as we are shaped and molded into those vessels that make Christ stand up at the right hand of the Father.

Acts 7:54–56:

> When they heard these things they were cut to the heart, and they gnashed at him with their teeth. But he, being full of the Holy Spirit, gazed into heaven and saw the Glory of God, and Jesus standing at the right hand of God and Stephen said, "Look! I see the heavens opened and the Son of Man standing at the right hand of God."

Beloved, Christ's appointed place is to be seated at the right hand of God, but Stephen's compliance to the faith engaged his behavior to preach the truth to the Pharisees and Sanhedrin council. In the face of certain death, he preached the Gospel of love in the presence of hate, and before he took his last breath on this earth, he said, "Lord do not charge them with sin." Then he fell asleep. "Hidden wars," let us begin.

Chapter 1

Spiritual Warfare

So, I find this law at work: Although I want to do good, evil is right there with me. For in my inner being I delight in God's law; but I see another law at work in me, waging war against the law of my mind and making me a prisoner of the law of sin at work within me. What a wretched man I am! Who will rescue me from this body that is subject to death? Thanks be to God, who delivers me through Jesus Christ our Lord! So then, I myself in my mind am a slave to God's law, but in my sinful nature a slave to the law of sin (Romans 7:21–25).

What Is It?

Spiritual warfare is the manifestation of conflict between two opposite forces, whether between countries, people, or doctrines like good and evil. The majority of Christians believe in some kind of evil being or force; they also believe this being or force attacks Christians from time to time. Their mindset in regard to spiritual warfare is that it is something that happens to Christians from time to time or something we struggle with when we want to do wrong. Due to Hollywood's misinformation agenda, many still believe it's a battle against demonic possession with the ritual of exorcisms being the weapon of choice. These attitudes and beliefs reveal an egotistical and self-indulged attitude toward the things of God. It suggests human beings, through carnal intelligence and strategies, can be victorious in times of spiritual conflict. Like the lone gunman of our imaginary past, we place ourselves in positions of power over spiritual warfare.

This mindset could not be more dangerously wrong. Spiritual warfare is not something that happens to us; it's the state we have been born into and is the continued state of the Christian's entire life. The above scriptures describe the inner conflict and turmoil man lives in and the daily battle he/she must fight for righteous living. In this environment, a false or arrogant assessment of one's self can be dangerous. If believers fail to properly recognize the constant hidden war raging within them, they run the risk of damaging important relationships, whether social, professional, intimate, or ultimately with self.

The premise of battle is to stop your opponent from their objective so you can fulfill your own, which makes warfare not just an open-ended conflict but conflict with an objective. Spiritual warfare, simply put, is the struggle between light and darkness.[2] Inside of the hearts and minds of Christians is the potential to perform and demonstrate great acts of patience, kindness, and love to others, but within that same heart is the potential to practice daily acts of impatience, cruelty, and hatred. The catalyst for either of these doctrines to be released are the *ethos* of the environments, circumstances, and situations in which we find ourselves. We are a people who walked in darkness and have seen a great light (Isa. 9:2), meaning we have been made aware of enlightened living versus our naturally dark, limited psychological perspectives. The objective of darkness is to have us always gravitate toward our psychology as we evaluate and access the ethos of environments, circumstances, and situations that confront us. The danger here is that natural weapons are useless in spiritual battles. It looks something like this:

---

2 Tim Clinton, Ron Hawkins, The Quick Reference Guide to Biblical Counseling personal and Emotional issues (Grand Rapids, MI: Baker Books. 2009), 234.

Case Study: Paula's Story

Paula, a forty-five-year-old young woman, who is the apple of her parents' eyes, is the oldest of three children. From an early age, she was taught the burden of responsibility, being the eldest child. These lessons came in the form of her parents' expectations, who thought she would set a good example for her younger siblings to follow. They expected her to sacrifice her desires and wants for her younger siblings, and assist her parents in caring for and babysitting her younger siblings. Paula was a good and obedient child; she learned these lessons well, and it benefitted her as she matured through college and in her professional and private life.

As Paula matured and advanced in her professional trajectory, she became bitter in her career and toward her colleagues. She felt they were selfish and inconsiderate. These feelings came from the early teachings of her parents who taught her to be the living example of good behavior, kind and compassionate to people, and always considerate. Paula was a good living representative of her company's promoted culture. What made her so miserable?

Nothing in her career came easy; she had to work hard and make many personal sacrifices, and no matter what she did, it always ended in heartache and never brought about her desired outcome. She started to think she shouldn't try anything new. She was unhappy and more resentful and did not know why.

We are told in scripture that wisdom is the principal thing; therefore, get wisdom. And in all your getting, get understanding (Prov. 4:7). Paula tried to live a good life and be considerate of everybody with the hope that it would be reciprocated. But, in a bad environment—an environment where selfish ambitions rule the day, where politics control the atmosphere, and combativeness, gossip, and disrespect dominate behavior, Paula, like most people in this environment, found herself fighting one battle on two fronts: the external front and the internal front. The external battle is easy to see and understand but requires serious spiritual discernment before any strategic move or counter moves is made. First John 4:1 says, "Beloved, do not believe every spirit, but test the spirit, whether they are of God; because many false prophets have gone out into the world." The internal battle is not-so-easy to identify because this requires surgical severing of personal and emotional feelings tied to our defense mechanisms. These emotions tend to short-circuit sound planning through kneejerk reactions. First John 2:15–16 says, "Do not love the world or the things in the world. If anyone loves the world, the love of the Father is not in him. For all that is in the world, the lust of the flesh, the lust of the eye, and the pride of life is not of the father but is of the world." This is the quagmire that Paula had to navigate herself out of. In this quagmire, you may hear yourself saying and thinking, *how could they do this to me? I treat everybody right. I am a good employee. I come to work every day even when am not feeling well;*

I come in early and stay late. I am good and productive at my job. Lord, how could you allow this to happen to me? These are the thoughts of a wounded and broken spirit. The events that initiate these kinds thoughts is always a traumatic eye-opening one that starts a chain reaction of self-doubt, mistrust, anger, and disgust toward your environment, your circumstances, and your situations. This is the middle of a spiritual battle, and ground zero of this battle will be how you continue to cooperate with expectations of the company as well as obey the doctrine of God.

The Purpose Behind It

As aforementioned, spiritual warfare is a struggle between light and darkness in the spiritual realm which manifests itself in the psychological and physical realm through attitudes and behavior. "Therefore rejoice, ye heavens, and ye that dwell in them! Woe to the inhabitants of the earth and of the sea! For the devil has come down unto you, having great wrath, because he knows that he has but a short time" (Rev. 12:12–13).

The foundation of hidden war is manipulation. Its purpose is to pull a person who is in the middle of the will of God, to abort their promise, shipwreck their faith, oppress the believer, confuse their direction, and stop their destiny. The warfare is a sophisticated attack designed to accomplish all of the aforementioned without leaving any traces of outside influences and the complete destruction of professional reputations, personal morality, judgment, and faith. It is often difficult for people of faith who try to live good lives to reconcile in their heart that they could be hated so much. Because most believers violate the Apostle Peter's instructions, we are never alert nor sober minded. Our faith in God is used as a psychological lift; we tend to use it as an us-against-them faith, with us being special, them being less than. This is why we so easily fall victim to this type of warfare through the entangling of sinful and rebellious responsive behavior toward the circumstances of life.

The Trauma of It

Suffering is the main symptom of hidden wars; this suffering is multifaceted. The apostle Paul describes it this way: "We are hard pressed on every side, but not crushed; perplexed, but not in despair; persecuted, but not abandoned; struck down, but not destroyed" (2 Cor. 4:8–9). Trauma manifests itself in people's lives both physically and psychologically. Both are harmful to us, but psychological trauma can be a life-killer; thus it is the foundation of Satan's hidden warfare. John 10:10 says, "The thief comes only to steal kill and destroy; I have come that they may have life and have it more abundantly."

Beloved, some events in life cause pain that goes deep and lasts a long time. These are traumas; a trauma would be considered a situation beyond our control, a spiritual or physical attack. One that shakes us to our core can lead to psychological or mental disorders or thoughts of suicide, and in most cases, the journey to recovery is slow and flashbacks of the event or events are common.[3] This attack is designed to overwhelm our adapting and coping mechanisms for life, so we make bad decisions and hurt other people, especially those close to us. This attack affects us so deeply that any ordinary response to danger continues to persist in an altered state long after the danger is over.[4]

The corporate culture at times can be a hostile place to its employees. Some may have great careers through social promotions given and salary plateaus reached, leading to new homes and affluent lifestyles, while at the same time, others will have careers ruined, reputations destroyed, and finances obliterated. The stakes are high, and most people liken it to a life-or-death battle. All Christians who are living their lives with a vision while they navigate the corporate culture are in the midst of a spiritual battle. If you have put

---

3   Tim Clinton, Ron Hawkins. *The Quick Reference Guide to Biblical Counseling Personal and Emotional issues* (Baker Books, 2009), 260.
4   Ibid., 260.

your trust in Jesus Christ, you are under attack. Many believers are unaware of the attack and chock it up to mean, evil, jealous people and or coworkers. Regardless of our awareness, we all engage in this battle.[5] And this battle feels real, even though most fighting will take place in the spirit realm while we launch carnal weapons of anger, resentment, bitterness, and profanity as a defense. Ephesians 6:12–13 says:

> For we do not wrestle against flesh and blood, but against the rulers, against the authorities, against the cosmic powers over this present darkness, against the spiritual forces of evil in the heavenly places. Therefore, take up the whole armor of God that you may be able to withstand in the evil day, and having done all, to stand firm.

This spiritual battle is so real that it can overwhelm

---

5   Ibid., Pg. 235

our emotions, distort our perspectives, and alter our temperament. People don't have this kind of power over each other, but the spiritual forces represented in this scripture are Satan and his minions who tempt, entice, provoke, and influence people in this present time to oppress others physically, emotionally, and spiritually. The one thing oppressed people fight for is their liberation, so how can liberation theology help the employee who believes he/she is being oppressed, occupationally, spiritually, and emotionally?

Liberation Theology

Liberation theology will be used as a methodology throughout this book as we seek to give answers to those who have believed the false advertisements and lies of the twentieth and twenty-first centuries, an ideology that tells us, "You can have whatever you want and have it all right now."

What is liberation theology? This theology can trace its roots back to the mid-twentieth century when Jurgen

Moltmann rose in status at the University of Tubingen and was influenced by the Marxist philosopher Ernst Bloch, which led to the development of the theology of hope.[6] Moltmann's theology is an extreme one as it tends not to focus on the risen Christ and the holy church, but how Christ and the church are affecting the future as it pertains to the poor and oppressed people of the world.

The more common and useful version of liberation theology was one called "black theology" by James H. Cone, professor of theology at Union Theological Seminary. Cone's version of liberation theology has also been named "black theology." The civil rights movement in America incorporated many tenants of "black theology" long before Cone introduced it to the world. This theology is founded on God's concern for the poor and oppressed people of the world.

Isaiah 61:1–3 says:

---

6   Paul Enns. *The Moody Handbook of Theology* (Moody Publishers, 1989), 635.

The Spirit of the Lord God is upon me; because the Lord has anointed me to preach good tidings unto the meek; he has sent me to bind up the brokenhearted, to proclaim liberty to the captives, and the opening of the prison to them that are bound; To proclaim the acceptable year of the Lord, and the day of vengeance of our God; to comfort all that mourn; to appoint unto them that mourn in Zion, to give unto them beauty for ashes, the oil of joy for mourning, the garment of praise for the spirit of heaviness; that they might be called trees of righteousness, the planting of the Lord, that he might be glorified.

People who feel oppressed, whether it be through war, imperialism, or an aggressive supervisor, have similar emotional and spiritual responses. Oppression produces trauma,which produces anger, and when anger is an automatic response to any situation, it is a primary emotional response. Anger can only be expressed in one of two ways: internalization or ventilation. The employee feeling oppressed by their boss and internalizing their anger will suffer from a variety of behavioral, personal, and emotional issues. This employee will wage a hidden war just to get out of bed and put on a mask of confidence and normalcy to make it through the day at a place they feel is the source of their torment.

One of the first and main issues/disorders that tends to plague a person in this battle is *discouragement*. When *discouragement* settles in, people start to melt away and lose themselves in doubt and hopelessness. You will notice a lack of confidence in self, a lack of confidence in God, and a lack of hope for the future. These dynamics normally dominate their perspectives and leave them in a constant state of sadness. This issue is a life-killer, for it can steal and destroy the present and future hope of a joyous life. The believer must hold on to the truth of God's Word, which says in Romans 8:28, "We know that all things work together for good to those who love God, who have been called according to His purpose."

Another issue present in employees who have suffered traumatic experiences at the hands of supervisors and jobs is *bitterness*. This disorder is also dangerous because it is a poisonous root that grows and creates an attitude of extended and intense anger and hostility, which almost always is followed by resentment and a desire to get even.[7]

When offenders and offenses go unforgiven and hurt and anger are allowed to grow, it poisons our nature. Often, employees who have been traumatized also display characteristics of *bitterness*. They may seem resentful toward their job or any job, constantly express thoughts of revenge, can be sarcastic among coworkers, critical through unkind remarks or comments, come across self-righteous, consistently in conflict with others, aggressive in relationships, and display controlling

---

7   Tim Clinton, Ron Hawkins. *The Quick Reference Guide to Biblical Counseling Personal and Emotional issues* (Baker Books, 2009), 47.

behavior. This sin also destroys life. Hebrews 12:14–15 says, "Make every effort to live in peace with everyone and to be holy; without holiness no one will see the Lord. See to it that no one falls short of the grace of God and that no bitter root grows up to cause trouble and defile many." Employees who find themselves in the grips of these emotional and behavioral issues will also struggle with anxiety and inconsistency in eating and sleep—all are signs of the effects of trauma on a person's life. So, the question remains, as the apostle Paul asked, "Who can deliver me from this?"

CHAPTER 2

LIBERATION

Jesus answered them, "Most assuredly, I say to you, whoever commits sin is a slave of sin. And a slave does not abide in the house forever, but a son abides forever. Therefore, if the Son makes you free, you shall be free indeed." (John 8:34–36).

L iberation: the act of setting someone free from imprisonment, slavery, oppression, limits, thoughts, and/or behaviors.

The Oppressor

Beloved, biblical theology tells us that a great and dangerous enemy has come down to Earth and we ought to be mindful of him. Revelation 12:12 says, "Therefore rejoice, you heavens and you who dwell in them! But woe to the earth and the sea because the devil has gone down to you! He is filled with fury, because he knows that his time is short."

All throughout human history Satan has been using people to destroy people and, in some cases, he uses multiple people to derail and destroy other people or groups of people. Egypt became a place of rest and peace for the Hebrew people until a thought was planted into the minds of the Egyptian people.

Exodus 1:8–12 says:

Now a new king arose over Egypt, who did not know Joseph. He said to his people, "Behold, the people of the sons of Israel are more and mightier than we. Come, let us deal wisely with them, or else they will multiply and in the event of war, they will also join themselves to those who hate us, and fight against us and depart from the land." So, they appointed taskmasters over them to afflict them with hard labor. And they built for Pharaoh Storage cities, Pithom and Rameses. But the more they afflicted them, the more they multiplied and the more they spread out, so that they were in dread of the sons of Israel. The Egyptians compelled the sons of Israel to labor rigorously; and they made their lives bitter with hard labor in mortar and bricks and at all kinds of labor in the field, all their labors which they rigorously imposed on them.

The story goes on to describe how overseers and

taskmasters were put over them to oppress and enslave them. The Philistines used Delilah to trap and subdue Samson the judge, which was their attempt to derail his assignment and the people's deliverance.

Judges 16:4–5 says, "Entice him, and find out where his great strength lies, and by what means we may overpower him, that we may bind him to afflict him; and every one of us will give you eleven hundred pieces of silver." King Herod's wife used her own daughter to have John the Baptist beheaded, this same John who Jesus said no man on Earth was greater than in heaven. Mark 6:21–24 says:

Then an opportune day came when Herod on his birthday gave a feast for his nobles, the high officers, and the chief men of Galilee. And when Herodias' daughter herself came in and danced, and pleased Herod and those who sat with him, the king said to the girl, "Ask me whatever you want, and I will give *it* to you." He also swore to her, "Whatever you ask me, I will give you, up to half my kingdom." So, she went out and said to her mother, "What shall I ask? And she said, "The head of John the Baptist."

This is an important doctrine to know and understand because it will be the difference between containing the hidden war internally or escalating it externally. Many oppressed people, including me, have been so emotionally hurt by an oppressor that we make them enemy number one. We psychologically allow them to grow bigger and stronger in our hearts and minds than they are. This is a key trigger for fear and anxiety. This fear, which is supposed to be a good thing because it helps us with our fight or flight decisions, becomes a bad thing as we are now fearing things in a psychological state that are not real or our fear is out of proportion to the real danger.[8]

---

8 Ibid., 117.

The Oppressed

Second Corinthians 4:7–10 says:

> But we have this treasure in jars of clay to show that this all-surpassing power is from God and not from us. We are hard pressed on every side, but not crushed; perplexed, but not in despair; persecuted, but not abandoned; struck down, but not destroyed. We always carry around in our body the death of Jesus, so that the life of Jesus may also be revealed in our body.

The twenty-first century oppressed saint must face hard realities about their relationship with Christ and their individual motives for wanting to proclaim Christianity and their relationship with Jesus in the world. This saint seems to enjoy the glory and majesty of quoting scripture and testifying how good God is to them, especially in times of trouble. The problem with this type of theology is it is not authentic but rather Pharisee-like in nature. The desire to let the world know the God of heaven, Abraham, Isaac, and Jacob is on your side without any display of trust or faith in Him represents an ideology and theology of self-achievement and self-accomplishment. It suggests a conjuring up of hope and help in times of trouble without the responsibility and accountability of understanding and living a life of faith, which, according to Hebrews 11:1, "is the substance of things hoped for, the evidence of things not seen."

The saint, whether in a corporate setting or not, should be consumed with the hope of the promise of salvation and the embracing of this new life. If this is done properly and truthfully, trials and tribulations won't be so paralyzing and crippling; emotional and behavioral issues won't take hold of our natures and change our characters. This is true liberation from our deliverer and liberator Jesus Christ.

The Liberator and Liberated

Isaiah 61:1–3 says:

> The Spirit of the Lord God is upon me; because the Lord has anointed me to preach good tidings unto the meek; he has sent me to bind up the brokenhearted, to proclaim liberty to the captives, and the opening of the prison to them that are bound; To proclaim the acceptable year of the Lord, and the day of vengeance of our God; to comfort all that mourn; to appoint unto them that mourn in Zion, to give unto them beauty for ashes, the oil of joy for mourning, the garment of praise for the spirit of heaviness; that they might be called trees of righteousness, the planting of the Lord, that he might be glorified.

The above scripture is a prophetic writing from the prophet Isaiah that details the foundational principle of Jesus Christ's ministry on Earth. The ecclesiastical doctrine of the church is based on "God sending His only begotten son to save us," and through this scripture, we see the doctrine of salvation, sanctification, and glorification being met. This doctrine in layman's terms is freedom, or to be more specific, "to be free." It represents a freedom from the influence of thoughts that can paralyze us, frighten us, create anxiety, discouragement, despair, and depression in our lives. So, when the oppressed saint feels delivered because God has changed their location from one company to another with a higher compensation package or from one demanding boss to an easy-going one, but not their mind, this theology is weak and not of God.

The apostle reminds us the type of relationship we ought to have with our Savior and the world. He says in Philippians 4:11–12:

> Not that I speak from want, for I have learned
> to be content in whatever circumstances I am.
> I know how to get along with humble means,

and I also know how-to live-in prosperity; in any and every circumstance I have learned the secret of being filled and going hungry, both of having abundance and suffering need. I can do all things through Him who strengthens me. Nevertheless, you have done well to share with me in my affliction.

This is a mind that is content, not with the trappings, enticements, or temptations of the world that seduce the lust of our eyes and flesh, but most importantly provides a platform for the pride of our lives. The source of this contentment is obedience to the direct will of God while not being distracted by His permissive will. God's direct will is to:

- Assemble with others in worship (Heb. 10:25);
- Be faithful in marriage (2 Cor. 6:14);
- Raise children by God's standards (Eph. 6:1-2);
- Obey and honor parents (1 Tim. 5:8);

- Support one's own family (Acts 1:8);
- Meditate on Scripture (Ps. 12); and
- Show love to others (1 Cor. 13).

Permissive will is what He allows to happen. Most of what we see every day is under God's permissive will.

- Building a new grocery store
- Falling interest rates
- Rising gas prices
- The termination, car accident, cancer diagnosis
- An election of a president
- Our choices we make to glorify Him or not

Here is where we see the twenty-first century saint woefully ill-prepared to adapt and cope with the emotional and spiritual assaults that take place on a daily basis in the corporate environment. Because most are distracted by the events that take place in God's permissive will, they vehemently reject their responsibility to God's direct will.

The theology of the Synoptic Gospels points both believer and nonbeliever to an understanding that saving faith comes by way of believing. You don't have to be circumcised, eat special diets, or give up any and all pleasures; just simply believe. Acts 10:43 says, "All the prophets testify about him that everyone who believes in him receives forgiveness of sins through his name."

This grace of God will not be given unto us without repentance; this dynamic is inextricably linked to saving faith. So, there is no liberation of the mind without faith in Christ, and faith is never bestowed without repentance. Acts 2:38 says, "Peter replied, 'Repent and be baptized, every one of you, in the name of Jesus Christ for the forgiveness of your sins. And you will receive the gift of the Holy Spirit.'"

There is an underlying theme of the Gospels written to the Jewish diaspora and those of us who call ourselves Christians. Like them, we are not an ethnic people, but rather a covenant nation; we are not identified by our race, language, dialect, or accent, but rather on our public relationship with Christ and others.

James 1:22–25 says:

> But be doers of the word, and not hearers only, deceiving yourselves. For if anyone is a hearer of the word and not a doer, he is like a man observing his natural face in a mirror; for he observes himself, goes away, and immediately forgets what kind of man he was. But he who looks into the perfect law of liberty and continues in it and is not a forgetful hearer but a doer of the work, this one will be blessed in what he does.

For the believer, the stakes are higher because the one thing that difficult people and environments affect first and most often is our psyche, which in turn, affects our perspectives, moods, and ultimately behaviors and decisions. If we are not careful, we, the liberated, could disconnect ourselves from our liberator through wrong understanding or insufficient knowledge. This hidden war between impulsive natural responses or quiet internal prayer and reflection is the battle between our faith and the manifestation of that faith in demonstrating kindness toward people without conditions, judgments, or hearsay.

The theology of the Gospel of James gives great insight into the corporate environment and its hierarchy. The apostle James wrote his letter to the twelve tribes who were dispersed abroad, but more specifically to the Jews who accepted Christ and were converted to Christendom. The letter was written to give them insight because within the assembly, carnality prevailed.[9] On the surface, James was addressing the division within the church between rich and poor, but underneath, he was speaking about wrong attitudes in the matter of money and oppression of poor or less-than people.

In our corporations today, a hierarchy exists and is

---

9   Paul Enns. *The Moody Handbook of Theology* (Moody Publishers, 1989), 12

rigorously enforced. It is based on titles, compensation, influence, and access. Those with the greater titles and higher compensation receive greater influence and access. The problem comes when this individual has a wrong attitude toward people with lower titles and compensation, no influence, and no access. James's epistle was written to correct carnal spirits that so easily arise in us when we begin to achieve our career goals. He describes the presence of partiality among the people based on material possession and the controlling of one's tongue. In corporate environments where power and money are wielded as powerful weapons to bring about desires, undermine systems, and hurt people, James's theology addresses where and why this comes about.

James 1:14 says, "But each person is tempted when they are dragged away by their own evil desire and enticed." Here we see the sin nature of fallen man at work; it is this lust that is the inner motivation and response to outer solicitations and stimuli that result in sinful and carnal behavior in both the assembly of God as well as in the corporate environment.[10] Liberation is not only for the oppressed, but also for the oppressor. People who are slaves to sin in the workforce almost always demonstrate the following characteristics from their nature:

- They tend to show partiality toward people they believe are useful to them;
- They fail to have compassion toward those who are not useful to them;
- They miss opportunities to do good; and
- They struggle with forgiveness.

When these dynamics clash, we see the declaration of *"hidden wars"* being signed in the hearts and minds of the oppressed.

---

10 Ibid., 105.

CHAPTER 3

FAITH

"Now faith is the substance of things hoped for, the evidence of things not seen." Hebrews 11:1

Soren Kierkegaard, the Danish philosopher, said, "Faith sees best in the dark."

What Is It?

As believers and nonbelievers live in the twenty-first century (or any century), we see the difficult struggles they endure to cope and adapt to the never-ending problems and issues of life in their homes, jobs, families, and marriages. How is faith used to help us overcome mental anguish and discouragement? The above scripture from the book of Hebrews tells us what faith truly is: it's being sure of whatever you are hoping for and confident in what we do not see. This concept runs counter to the natural mind, as most people only truly see God in the rearview mirror rather than the wind- shield. Many Christians give great testimonies and weak prophesies, in that their testimonies are so grand, absolute, and confident in comparison to an uncertain future where we are trusting the same God of our testimony to bring us through uncertain situations and circumstances unscathed.

Yet, are we trusting Him? In this "hidden war," our enemy's main purpose and desire is to get us to doubt and lose trust and faith in God and take matters into our own hands, through stress, worry, and a consuming nature, which leads to burnout and sickness. Remember Satan's conversation with God about Job in Job 1:10–12?

Have you not made a hedge about him and his house and all that he has, on every side? You have blessed the work of his hands, and his possessions have increased in the land. "But put forth Your hand now and touch all that he has; he will surely curse You to Your face." Then the Lord said to Satan, "Behold, all that he has is in your power, only do not put forth your hand on him." So, Satan departed from the presence of the Lord.

Beloved, Satan was wrong about Job to a point, but

Job did suffer real traumatic events that affected his relationship and trust in God. Most of us will never have to go through a "Job experience," but we all have our own crosses to carry. The official definition of psychological or emotional trauma in layman's terms is any type of damage to your mind due to severely distressing events. When we become overwhelmed by the issues of life and our ability to cope and adapt to those issues become ineffective, trauma begins to affect our minds. The foundation of many disorders in people's lives are the experiences of traumatic events.

In the twenty-first century, people view jobs, salaries, and the benefits they come with as a necessity to life. So, if they are threatened, it becomes a life-threatening, traumatic event. As long as these things are seen in this manner, any and all threats to them become catastrophic events. Most people never experience physical life-threatening events, but almost all experience traumatic situations that include threats to employment. People liken this to imminent death or serious injury to them and their families.[11]

How and Where Does It Work?

Individuals experiencing trauma feel entirely out of control and respond with understandable fear, helplessness, or horror. Most importantly, the victim will typically experience the event over and over again in the form of flashbacks and nightmares. This repetitive process hardens neural pathways in the brain that become easy to be triggered when similar events are recognized.[12] So how can faith help us when it looks like Satan is using people and our own minds to destroy us?

The first thing about faith is it's substantive; it is real and empirical whereas emotional and psychological trauma is not. It's a reliving of events in the mind that produces stress in the physical body. So the first line of defense in this "hidden war" is to identify what is

---

11 W. Brad Johnson, William L. Johnson. *The Minister's Guide to Psychological Disorders and Treatments* (Routledge Publisher, 2014), 90.
12 Ibid., 90.

real and what is not; if we are constantly responding to events and situations from our past and not seeing or accepting our present reality, we now become victims of Satan's plan in 2 Corinthians 4:4: "The god of this age has blinded the minds of unbelievers, so that they cannot see the light of the gospel that displays the glory of Christ, who is the image of God." Then, we are no longer living by faith or trusting in God, but rather, through impulsive insecure thinking that can now move this war from the internal battlefield to an external one.

The apostle Paul constantly instructs us on how we must walk and live. Second Corinthians 5:7 says, "For we walk by faith, not by sight," and Romans 1:17 says, "For in it the righteousness of God is revealed from faith to faith; as it is written, 'The just shall live by faith.'" How is this done? As mentioned before, we must have a good grasp of our reality in the world while simultaneously understanding our relationship with God. Then, we must always have our eyes on Christ no matter what comes into our minds. Hebrews 12:1–2 says:

Therefore we also, since we are surrounded by so great a cloud of witnesses, let us lay aside every weight, and the sin which so easily ensnares us, and let us run with endurance the race that is set before us, looking unto Jesus, the author and finisher of our faith, who for the joy that was set before Him endured the cross, despising the shame, and has sat down at the right hand of the throne of God.

So, in addition to being confident in what we do not see, faith is also, and most importantly, putting everything in God's hands and letting Him tell us what to do.[13] As a Christian pastor and professional counselor, I realize implementing this mindset into a lifestyle can be difficult, especially if you are a smart person who trusts in your own abilities to understand tasks and accomplish them. This behavior and thought

---

13 Jerry Falwell. *Building Dynamic Faith* (Thomas Nelson Publisher, 2005), 35

process must be rejected because human achievement will never bring about the righteousness of God and only helps to promote man's arrogance and independence from God, and won't develop us into people who will continually learn to walk by faith. In trying to defeat and over- come spiritual attacks through carnal means only reveals how little faith we truly have. The late Dr. Jerry Falwell, founder of the Thomas Road Baptist Church and Liberty University, said:

> You will overcome some problems in this life quickly, completely, and triumphantly. But some obstacles may eat at you like slowly rotting timbers for the rest of your life. Some problems will crash into you head-on and hurt you, or even permanently maim you. Some problems you may never defeat. That's not necessarily lack of faith.[14]

---

14 Ibid., 191.

The apostle Paul was a man familiar with arrogance and driven by human achievement. About himself, he said in 2 Corinthians 12:7–10:

And lest I should be exalted above measure by the abundance of the revelations, a thorn in the flesh was given to me, a messenger of Satan to buffet me, lest I be exalted above measure. Concerning this thing I pleaded with the Lord three times that it might depart from me. And He said to me, "My grace is sufficient for you, for My strength is made perfect in weakness." Therefore, most gladly I will rather boast in my infirmities, that the power of Christ may rest upon me. Therefore, I take pleasure in infirmities, in reproaches, in needs, in persecutions, in distresses, for Christ's sake. For when I am weak, then I am strong.

Man's sinful nature will always seek his own glory and deny God of His, which is why God had to instruct

Gideon about whittling his thirty-two thousand army down to three hundred. With God, you will either fight by faith or not at all. He will not let us take His glory so we can brag that we had a hand in our own deliverance. Many people feel helpless in the corporate environment of office politics and the ethos of the supervisor-to-subordinate dynamic. In this reality, we find individuals believing they have no option, no hope, and no future, but here are some principles that we ought to keep in mind when we feel like we are not making progress in a fight against an enemy:

- You are winning an inner battle just because you've entered the fight because the war is first won on the inside.

- Keep fighting when you're right, not just successful. Don't fight for vanity or material success; we fight for truth, influence, and the cessation of evil.

- Know that some battles are not winnable, but speak up and stand up. The victory may be in the eventuality rather in the immediate. John the Baptist was beheaded, Jesus was crucified, Paul was decapitated by Nero's command. Thomas was scourged bind together then crucified before he died. Peter was crucified upside down. The point here is that all of these battles seemed lost until you look at the eventuality and totality of the Christian faith, then we realize they won.

- Keep your eyes on Christ and not the battle or your enemy. Spiritual wars are never won with carnal weapons.

- Know why you are fighting. Whose battle is it: yours or God's?

Why Do Believers Need It?

You may have heard the old saying "I never promised

you a rose garden." As common as this quote is, in the Kingdom of God, it may be vitally important for us to remember. Many saints who believe in God and His Son Jesus Christ want to do so desperately. They want to serve Him and know they are pleasing to Him. But most also want a conditional relationship with Him, something that can be measured and quantified, or better yet, negotiated. We sinners always want to have some say in everything that goes on around us, even when we have no clue what those things are. Here is where the above quote and faith will meet to make us better as believers in Christ. This world would be a beautiful place if we never failed, everyone got along peacefully, food and money were in an abundance, wars and racial hatred were nonexistent, and hospitals had a pill for every disease under the sun.

Beloved, this utopia belongs in our dreams and fantasies because the real world is full of problems, tragedies, and violence. People steal from one another—including believers; we all get sick, frustrated, discouraged, depressed, and more, now than ever before, burned-out. Politicians lie, steal, and commit adultery on their wives and husbands, and the church is divided among racial and political lines. This is where we find ourselves and why we so desperately need to live and walk by faith to help us to cope, adapt, trust, and believe while living through the realities of life's issues. Tragedy and human calamity are a built-in part of life, but believers who are believers in appearance only—of whom I call "schizophrenic saints." Because they are intelligent people but can't get past their own limited understanding in the matters of faith, their belief and behavior are never aligned; they can't reconcile the real struggles and issues of life and their limited understanding of the Divine and His purpose, will, and way. So, this type of saint tends to be extremely weak and unfaithful when wrestling with the ups and downs of life, especially when dealing with deeply ingrained behavioral and emotional responses to the issues of life. They tend to struggle with forgiveness, acceptance of seasons, and faith in the eventuality of their own lives. They focus heavily on the immediate shock and trauma of current circumstance and situation, and reject the age-old response from the "holy writ."

Exodus 1:12–13 says:

> Is this not the word that we spoke to you in Egypt, saying, "Leave us alone that we may serve the Egyptians"? For it would have been better for us to serve the Egyptians than to die in the wilderness. But Moses said to the people, "Do not fear! Stand still and see the salvation of the Lord which He will accomplish for you today; for the Egyptians whom you have seen today, you will never see them again. The Lord will fight for your battles if you only will be still."

When people who are unaccustomed to trusting God and others when it comes to their own deliverance are put in circumstances where their strength, connections, or brilliance isn't enough to deliver them, they get childlike in their emotions and behavior. Hostility and resentment tend to present an immature attitude of the day. It takes faith to stand still when you feel the world is against you, your name is being slandered, your reputation is being sullied, and no one cares about you. So, in a nutshell, we need faith and the righteous of God to keep our minds stayed on Christ and in perfect peace.

Is It Needed in the Twenty-First Century?

2 Timothy 3:1–6:

> This know also, that in the last days perilous times shall come. For men shall be lovers of their own selves, covetous, boasters, proud, blasphemers, disobedient to parents, unthankful, unholy, without natural affection, trucebreakers, false accusers, incontinent, fierce, despisers of those that are good, Traitors, heady, high-minded, lovers of

pleasures more than lovers of God having a form of godliness but denying the power thereof: from such turn away. For of this sort are they which creep into houses, and lead captive silly women laden with sins, led away with divers' lusts.

The scriptures describe perfectly the ethos of the environment and people that Christians will have to work around and live among. In these environments, the doctrine of self rules dominates the atmospheric conditions. People will be consumed with self, their problems, their achievements, their battles, their accomplishments. This will all be driven by a never-ending engine, fueled by ego. Even the holiness of scripture will be used and manipulated to boost one's own status in both the real and cyber worlds of social media, of which will be full of postings and pictures of their own lives enjoying exotic vacations, meeting rich and famous people, and living in a state of perpetual happiness.

Is faith needed in these times? You bet it is; these times represent an illusion of life and not real life. The art of conversing and connecting is fast fading into the archives of "old school" while this illusion of life dominates the minds of the weak and holds them captive to the images of how things look rather than how they are. Now faith is what you have until you get what you want; it's that power of belief that keeps and sustains in the midst of hopelessness and discouragement.

Hebrews 11:27–38:

> By faith he left Egypt, not fearing the wrath of the king; for he endured, as seeing Him who is unseen. By faith he kept the Passover and the sprinkling of the blood, so that he who destroyed the firstborn would not touch them. By faith they passed through the Red Sea as though they were passing through dry land; and the Egyptians, when they attempted it, were drowned. By faith the walls of Jericho fell down after they had

been encircled for seven days. By faith Rahab the harlot did not perish along with those who were disobedient, after she had welcomed the spies in peace. And what more shall I say? For time will fail me if I tell of Gideon, Barak, Samson, Jephthah, of David and Samuel and the prophets, who by faith conquered kingdoms, performed acts of righteousness, obtained promises, shut the mouths of lions, quenched the power of fire, escaped the edge of the sword, from weakness were made strong, became mighty in war, put foreign armies to flight. Women received back their dead by resurrection; and others were tortured, not accepting their release, so that they might obtain a better resurrection; and others experienced mocking's and scourging's, yes, also chains and imprisonment. They were stoned, they were sawn in two, they were tempted, they were put to death with the sword; they went about in sheepskins, in goatskins, being destitute, afflicted, ill-treated men of whom the world was not worthy, wandering in deserts and mountains and caves and holes in the ground.

Yes, beloved, faith is a vital part of life, for each and every one will be tested in their life; we will all have some battles to fight. Some we will win and a lot we'll lose, but by faith we can all endure to the promise. In these perilous times not only will men be lovers of themselves, but they will spend a significant amount of time trying to persuade people that they aren't and they want the best for everyone. Faith not only sustains us, but it keeps us anchored in Christ while we wait in hope for what we prayed for, so we are not turned upside down and inside out by the storms of life and the characters who come to intimidate, manipulate, and dominate the downtrodden. This type of environment can do serious mental, emotional, and spiritual damage to the faint of heart and those whose faith is weak or nonexistent.

We can so easily get ensnared in the viciousness of the culture and become like our oppressors—get depressed, lethargic, bitter, resentful, angry, and critical with people to the point that it changes our personalities for the worse. First Corinthians

15:33–34 says, "Do not be deceived: 'Bad company corrupts good morals.' Become sober-minded as you ought and stop sinning; for some have no knowledge of God. I speak this to your shame." When our morality gets corrupted by hostile environments, know we are in jeopardy of losing this hidden war in our hearts, which will manifest itself in our attitudes and behaviors.

CHAPTER 4

LOVE

1 John 4:7 "Beloved, let us love one another; for love is of God, and every one that loves is born of God and knows God."

Types of Biblical Love

Storge: A natural and instinctive love, as between a parent and a child.

1 Corinthians 13:4–7:

Love is patient, love is kind. It does not envy, it does not boast, it is not proud. It does not dishonor others, it is not self-seeking, it is not easily angered, it keeps no record of wrongs. Love does not delight in evil but rejoices with the truth. It always protects, always trusts, always hopes, always perseveres.

Phileo: A self-sacrificial love as between friends.

Romans 12:10: "Love one another with brotherly affection. Outdo one another in showing honor."

Mark 12:31: "The second is this: 'You shall love

your neighbor as yourself.' There is no other commandment greater than these."

Eros: This type of love can be deceiving, and the Bible limits it to the covenant of marriage. Outside of the bounds of marriage, it can be lustful, possessive, and selfish. It is motivated by fulfilling the sexual desires of the flesh.

> Matthew 5:28: "But I tell you that anyone who looks at a woman lustfully has already committed adultery with her in his heart."

Agape is the highest form of love; the love that does not need conditions to be activated. It is God's love.

> John 3:16: "For God so loved the world, that he gave his only Son, that whoever believes in him should not perish but have eternal life."

So, if faith is vital to keep us focused on God and His promise, then love is essential to always be the representative of our souls, characters, and behaviors. Love is representative of our faith. Our faith and love are given to us by God, but where faith is for us, our love is for others.

Let's examine this for a minute. As people of faith, we are called to live at a more mature level of existence than we did before we became involved in an intimate relationship with Christ. The perfect place to test and practice this belief system is in the workplace because here is where we find all kinds of people from different races, cultures, education levels, genders, and ages. We must also include alternate-lifestyle individuals. In such a diverse environment, both your faith and love will be tested, and this test is the war that will discourage your faith and wax your love cold. The ultimate victory in this arena is, can we remain faithful to God's commands and not our own feelings and perspectives, and can we trust God enough to know the faith and love He has given us is more than enough to change any situation and circumstance if we know what to look for?

Storge Love

This natural and selfless love is normally associated between the bond of a parent and a child and holds the key to solving most of the world's relational problems. The only question is, are we mature enough to apply it in our lives? This type of love is such a powerful and transformational dynamic in human interaction that it scares most of us from even thinking about it in our circumstances. It is almost always rejected as being weak or having hidden agendas or that others will take advantage of us if we are seen in this light.

It can be best summed up in the message from 1 Corinthians 13. Here, we find the apostle Paul laying out the magnitude, power, and importance of storge love. He begins with the comparison of human achievement and accomplishments because humanity will often try to use their accomplishments as a substitute for loving and caring for each other's wellbeing. He starts with our speech and our insatiable appetite to brag, boast, and hear ourselves talk. This activity is done for selfish gain and comes across as noise, and in some cases, bothersome noise. Then he goes to human intellect and our abilities to comprehend, retain, and speak about the knowledge we have learned, and the faith we have in it. Without selfless love, it profits nothing; it gives us no value with people.

In the real world of human interaction, most people will never fully understand what you feel proud about in our conversations about accomplishments. They may never fully grasp the details about our occupations and industries, like the difference between a cyst or a lipoma or certifications or college degrees. But they will almost certainly know when you are genuinely interested in them and their life and the level of commitment you are willing to give them.

First Obstacle

So, here is the rub that starts a thought process in the hearts and minds of employees/people. When employees feel their work or any relationships with their jobs and bosses or others are one-sided and their needs are always sacrifices, their family's needs must always take a backseat to the job. Weekend baseball will be missed because Daddy or Mommy has to go to work because the company is not hiring due to attrition and is short-staffed. Cost of living increases will not be given because the company didn't meet its financial goals, yet still they purchased new equipment and office computers to increase productivity.

I have cited some common circumstances that get conversations at the water cooler started. Some of these situations may be easier to accept if compensation was involved, but what if you are a non- union employee or an at-will staff member? The feeling of abuse begins to form like distant clouds in your mind, only getting darker and darker. No one likes to be on the other end of the feelings of unfairness, especially if they feel that they have done all they can to be a good example and representation of their company.

Before I go on, I want to tak a minute to explore why these easily fixable, low-hanging fruit are allowed to mushroom and cause such divisive resentment in corporations. When we begin to take other people for granted or as less-than in the work environment, we are also taking their families for granted and less-than. This immature and imbecilic mindset represents insecure leadership, inexperienced leadership, and most importantly, selfish leadership. Any one of these types of leaderships is enough to bring major problems to the workforce. Unfair work practices create another dynamic in the workforce, and that's the feeling of betrayal. As previously mentioned, employees who pride themselves on playing by the rules of time and attendance, sound competency, and productivity tend to feel personally betrayed by their supervisors or bosses when the quality of their work is not taken into consideration. Feelings of betrayal can be a powerful motivator to drive out *storge* love and usher in thoughts and feelings of ill-will inside the hearts of the betrayed. Even on this side of the equation, we find immaturity and spoiled, bratty perspectives and behaviors.

When you have been victimized by betrayal on your job, it means somewhere along the way, you have exposed too much of yourself on the job and not discerned the nature of those you allowed to come in.

The Nature of Man

The nature of man represents a complex intangible system of the essence of humanity. Psychology and theology confront a complex task in attempting to understand human nature.[15] Consider the diverse perspectives on this topic offered by two literary authors. First, the often-misunderstood lines of Shakespeare's Hamlet:

---

15 David N, Entwistle. *Integrative Approaches to Psychology and Christianity* (Cascade Books, 2015), 142.

What a piece of work is a man! How noble in reason! How infinite in faculties, in form and moving how express and admirable! In action how like an angel! In apprehension how like god! The beauty of the world! The paragon of animals; and yet to me, what is this quintessence of dust? Man delights not me: no, nor woman.

And the second is Samuel Clemens (Mark Twain). In the words of the "Old Man" in his essay "What is Man?":

Man, the machine man the impersonal engine. Whatsoever a man is, is due to his make, and the influences brought to bear upon it by his heredities, his habits, his associations. He is moved, directed, commanded, by exterior influences solely. He originates nothing, not even thought.[16]

---

16 Ibid, 142.

Hamlet points out the inconsistencies in humanity that produces the character of Mother Teresa on one end and Adolf Hitler on the other. As human beings, we struggle to understand people can be blessed with such incredible abilities while at the same time be prone to such great evil. We can also be faithful to our jobs but not so much in our marriages and commitments. This reflects an immature mind and nature—one that only feels great when others are worshipping at our altars, telling us, "It's all going to be all right; you're too blessed too be stressed; God's got you," and so on.

The goal of psychology has always been to increase knowledge and the improvement of human life by the reduction of suffering or the optimizing of conditions under which human beings flourish.[17] Yet, psychology faces powerful enemies that hinder it from fulfilling its goals, with enemies like arrogance, pride, desire for recognition, and other failings. Christian theology

---

17 Ibid, 147.

approaches human nature from a different perspective; it believes God's revealed Word is discernable and is a guide for faith and its practice. It teaches that though humans were created in the image and likeness of God, they are still fallen beings. This should bring about an understanding that God's Word has the final say in the life of the Christian, not man. Theology does not try to alleviate suffering, but rather teach us how to live above it, cope with it, and adapt to it.

As Christians in the workplace, we live difficult lives unintentionally; our faith is based on this feast, famine, and sin/salvation doctrine. This doctrine keeps us always shackled to our nemesis. We hate our circumstances, pray for God to remove it from us or us from it; then after He hears our cries and responds to our pain, we take that same problem into our new space in our emotions, spirit life, and professional life. We can never move on; it's all we are passionate and detailed in talking about. "Why did it happen to me? How could God allow it? I want God to punish them for what they did to me. How could I possibly forgive this offense?" These are the painful thoughts of a mind leaning more on psychology and not enough on Christ.

Let us look at an old Sunday school illustration called "Fact, Faith, and Feelings." Visualize a train on a track. The engine represents the fact, that is, the truth of God's Word. The middle cabin car depicts our faith, our ability to choose; and the caboose characterizes our feelings and emotional life. Only the engine can pull the train forward; the caboose cannot move it at all. Thus, our decision-making capability (the middle car) must choose where it will place its faith. Will it be in the engine (God's truth) or in the caboose (human feelings)?[18] These are natural, and in some cases, needed emotions to explore, but they can also be the reason why we may never receive healing and restoration because reliving past events without a plan or purpose is nothing more than post-traumatic stress disorder

---

18 Charles, Allen Kollar. *Solution-Focused Pastoral Counseling* (Zondervan, 1997), 89.

out of control that can bring about flashbacks of past painful circumstances in any situation and cripple us in places we are supposed to be thriving in. Beloved, this is the perfect weapon used in a perfect attack, as cancer is the body's own cells mutating to attack itself. Here we find our minds, emotions, and feelings altered to attack our peace, hope, joy, and destiny.

CHAPTER 5

THE BATTLE

Matthew 11:12 "And from the days of John the Baptist until now the kingdom of heaven suffers violence, and the violent take it by force."

Like with anything in life, understanding is the key to success. Scripture teaches us in Proverbs 4:7, "Wisdom is the principal thing; therefore, get wisdom: and with all your getting get understanding." It says, no matter what state, situation, or circumstance you find yourself in, have a clear understanding of what you are encountering and observing. In our societies today, we have engineered a global economy with its own global marketplace, with the intentions to bring people together as a global community to solve a myriad of world problems like communicable disease, famine, war, climate change, hate, and poverty. As we all try to fit into this social setting, there are some key characteristics that must be defeated in the human psyche for this social experiment to work. So, let's look at where this battle for dominance of our spirit and psyche will be fought.

The Battlefield: Our Minds and Our Environments

There is something deeply disturbing about our desires

to do good to and for people while simultaneously practicing behavior to kill another's character, reputation, and or livelihood. This kind of internal struggle is not always noticeable to us when we are in the midst of it, which only motivates our reasons to continue in this hypocrisy. Pretending to be something has always been man's greatest challenge—who are we, what kind of people do we desire to be, and to whom will we be the most authentic version of ourselves?

The apostle Paul recognized his inability to win this war. Romans 7:19–24 says:

> For the good that I would I do not: but the evil which I would not, that I do. Now if I do that I would not, it is no more I that do it, but sin that dwelleth in me. I find then a law, that, when I would do good, evil is present with me. For I delight in the law of God after the inward man: But I see another law in my members, warring against the law of my mind,

and bringing me into captivity to the law of sin which is in my members. O wretched man that I am! who shall deliver me from the body of this death?

We see in this depiction the law of knowing what is right and doing what is right is not always mutually exclusive. The natural law to do what we feel based on how we perceive always seems stronger. The human mind is ground zero of this battle, and our environments can become allies to our enemy. Many times, this war is being fought long after a traumatic event has past. Stephen L. Carter, in his book, *Civility*, says:

So, I know psychologist say that nasty personal comments circumvent the higher parts of the brain, stirring to action something more atavistic. I know sociologists argue that a verbal attack is a form of definition of a group, marking the target as an outsider, and so is intended to alienate. I know postmodern insist that offensive, harassing words are a culturally permitted form of violence. And I know theologians condemn gratuitous insults as a sin against God's gift of speech. All of these strike me as fancy ways of saying that insulting people is wrong. But none of them influenced my decision not to attack my opponent.[19]

The human mind or psyche is a wonderful and powerful creation of God that resides in the human spirit. It is the intangible essence of who we are as nonphysical *and* physical beings. Yet, our minds, as powerfully impressive as they are, also have many weaknesses; they must be constantly renewed from worldly stimuli so the connection with the divine is never broken. Romans 12:2 says, "Do not be conformed to this world, but be transformed by the renewing of your mind, that by testing you may discern what is the will of God, what is good and acceptable and perfect."

The mind can be deceived by craftiness, tempted by lust, and enticed by lies. 2 Corinthians 11:3 says,

---

19 Stephen, L. Carter, *Civility Manners, Moral, and the Etiquette of Democracy* (Harper Perennial, 1998), 117.

"But I am afraid that as the serpent deceived Eve by his cunning, your thoughts will be led astray from a sincere and pure devotion to Christ." It operates best in peace and worst in confusion and strife. Philippians 4:7 says, "And the peace of God, which surpasses all understanding, will guard your hearts and your minds in Christ Jesus."

Throughout human history, man has always struggled to live in harmony with his environment and fellow man; he's always been at odds with balancing his own desires, wants, and needs with others and his environment. In pre-industrial times, he battled the elements, animals, and insects to produce sustainable crops for commerce and sustenance. The dynamics of this battle wreaks havoc on the human mind and psyche because our minds perceived it as a threat to our existence. We may associate one bad single event and apply it broadly to all seasons.

In human relationships, like our relationship with our environment, we tend to want to meet and satisfy our primary need in these relationships. With the environment, we want well-balanced, pest-free weather and with people, we want considerate, respectful friendships. Yet, if our minds are misled to the point that we need a particular person for a friend because we love them or want to be around them, and if this friend is irresponsible and inconsiderate with your friendship, the need to have this person as a friend will blind you from seeing who this person may truly be: a user and abuser of your needs.

So, when we get hurt in these types of relationships by friends, family members, or coworkers, we lose trust in all people and lump them all into the category of untrustworthy enemies without even considering our own immature decision-making process. This is a classic attack on our minds, which is designed to destroy our relationships with people and God while making us feel like victimized people who God wronged, and will continue to do wrong us, so our thinking is justified. This is the way God views human thoughts as troubled, easily manipulated, always unreliable, and rebellious to the Kingdom vision. Because, at the core of this manipulation are demonic influences. All human beings' thoughts are almost always motivated by their feelings and how it affects them positively or negatively. This is because the majority of human thoughts are focused on self; where we are thinking about ourselves and our place in the world, or more importantly, our place in our world. *Are we being treated fairly? Did we treat someone fairly? Will our dreams and aspirations come to pass and bring fulfillment to our lives? Is our family secure physically, financially, emotionally?* Our thoughts seem to be about us in connection to the world around us, and this sounds reasonable, but because the world around us is always in transition and upheaval, our thoughts reflect this uneasy, unstable, insecure pathology, which completely alters our psychology and the essence of us.

The world has a consistent story but not a consistent reality; the stories of most societies for its citizens are to be law-abiding, productive, faithful, patriotic members of said society. These stories are enforced through social norms, company policies, and public legislation, so violations of any of these can lead to societal ostracizing, progressive discipline, and criminal penalties. The reality is not so clear-cut, as violations of these stories are committed daily like corporate leadership engaging in sexual harassment, nepotism, and illegal and immoral behaviors that go unchecked and unpunished. An example is the public police officer who physically brutalizes, maims, and/or kills a citizen unjustly; or the corrupt public official who votes against the public good in favor of private enterprise. If a person's mind believes in the world systems and carries deep affections for it and then becomes a victim to these types of unstable upheavals, it can shatter the human spirit and alter the person forever.

The young employee who plays by the rules, went to school and earned a master's in business administration (MBA), only to find themselves ten years later still in the same position, underpaid and having to report to others who are less qualified than they are, will most likely feel like the world system lied to them and that career advancement and salary increases are not based on merit, but more on favors, family connections, and a willingness to compromise one's standards. The danger with this employee and the reason they will lose more than career dissatisfaction is because they have made the critical mistake to associate career and career advancement with a significant part of their happiness and satisfaction with work. This pathology has the real potential to be carried with this person throughout their professional career unless they learn how to recognize triggers that lead to past memories, which can adversely affect present decisions.

One of the questions I've always asked clients is, "Are your memories greater than your dreams?" The answer reveals a lot about a person, their journey, their perspective, and their hope. However, there is another crucial factor to the answers people give, and that's the distance they have traveled and where they are currently on the journey of life. Because human beings tend to be conditional beings, our answers tend to be based on the current circumstances of our lives. If we are going through a bad storm that won't end, we long for the carefree, less-stressful days of youth where our only worries were on us and our immediate needs. If life is storm-free in the present and plans are coming together, we tend to feel pretty good about our life and purpose; we look to the future with great anticipation and resolute faith.

Scripture teaches us in Hebrews 11:1, "Now faith is the substance of things hoped for, the evidence of things not seen." So, if our hope is so affected by the seen circumstances of life in the world, where is our true faith? If times are hard and full of disappointments and our faith leads us to seek easier times, is this faith? If times are great and fulfilling and it inspires us to joy and praise, is this faith? We must always remember that the past has gone and the future has not arrived, so let's live in the present, for the Word of God is present right now and He is an ever-present help in the times of trouble.

This is why we have been instructed to walk by faith and not by sight. The storms of life come in many forms—some come with specific purposes while others happen to us when we make certain decisions or no decisions at all. Life comes with built-in storms, but all storms have the potential to disrupt and discourage our purpose.

Let's take a look at an example of a disrupting storm. It's a scenario involving the Hebrew people and the long-awaited return to their Promised Land. It is in Ezra 4:1–5:

Now when the adversaries of Judah and Benjamin heard that the descendants of the captivity were building the temple of the Lord God of Israel, they came to Zerubbabel and the heads of the fathers' houses, and said to them, "Let us build with you, for we seek your God as you do; and we have sacrificed to

Him since the days of Esarhaddon king of Assyria, who brought us here." But Zerubbabel and Jeshua and the rest of the heads of the fathers' houses of Israel said to them, "You may do nothing with us to build a house for our God; but we alone will build to the Lord God of Israel, as King Cyrus the king of Persia has commanded us." Then the people of the land tried to discourage the people of Judah. They troubled them in building, and hired counselors against them to frustrate their purpose all the days of Cyrus king of Persia, even until the reign of Darius king of Persia.

The foundation of this storm was jealousy and envy, as the Hebrew's were the rightful and lawful owners of the land before they were exiled into captivity. In the seventy-year absence, the land was resettled by the Babylonians, who mixed and intermarried with Hebrew women, as the captives began to return with a steadfast purpose to resettle the land, rebuild their temple to God, and serve Him. The new settlers asked to be part of the building, as they knew something about the Hebrew faith from the women they married. The offer was rejected, and they were not recognized as part of the faith.

A specific piece of envy is the desire to take away from a person what brings them satisfaction, pleasure, and peace. If the envious person can't have and enjoy it, no one will. This kind of storm consists mainly of lies, character defaming, false accusations, and by bearing false witness. As the scripture points out, they hired lawyers to write reports to the king, accusing them of wasting money, treasonous behavior, and misappropriating funds for personal cost rather than national cost. This storm worked, as the people abandoned the temple project out of frustration, and it laid in waste and ruins for sixteen years. While they focused on building their own homes and lives, their eyes became accustomed to seeing the temple of their God lying in ruins.

Past memories can rob us of our purpose and zeal

until they become unrecognizable to us. Traumatic past memories tend to linger in our minds forever with the occasional interruption of our present plans and future imaginations, just to remind us of what happened to us, "Don't get too happy and comfortable because it can happen again." In the psychological world, we call this fear and anxiety disorder.

The Battle Plan: Distraction, Disillusionment, Discouragement

The entire battle plan is to introduce and maximize doubt in a person's life, doubt in our mind, friends, family, self, and even God. One of the best ways to bring about self-doubt is to be filled with envy and jealousy. These two siblings are the perverse children of a toxic mix of anger, anxiety-based insecurity, and an obsessive habit of comparing oneself, usually poorly, with others. There is also a root of fear in most jealousy—for instance, the fear of losing the love or praise of one's object of love or affection, while envy wants what someone else has.

Jealousy is being fearful that something one has attained will be taken. Jealousy also involves a triangle of three people, one of which is the jealous person becoming fixated on a usually misperceived rival, who is viewed as competing for the attention of the third person. Song of Solomon 8:6 says that love as "strong as death will produce powerful jealousy that is as cruel as the grave."

Envy may also be defined as "wanting what someone else has, whether it is status, possessions, lifestyle, relationships, or characteristics." This first attack distracts us from us our life, goals, dreams, and hopes. This time-tested disorder has been around since the biblical story of Cain and Abel. As the disparity between the haves and have-nots increase, the competition to achieve and maintain wealth, status, and financial standards of living have become increasingly dire; politics plays a more prevalent role in who the haves and have-nots are.

We see pandemic levels of distracted people suffering from envy and jealousy. The distraction comes from being dissatisfied with God's provision for our lives. These distracted people only see what God *hasn't* provided rather than what God *has* provided. It also comes from comparing themselves with others. US society has historically conditioned its citizens to see themselves only in comparison to others. These comparisons take on high stakes as they are directly attached to status and income-earning power as we make comparisons on intelligence, beauty, and/or attractiveness and popularity. This distraction runs deep and can consume a person's life because envy and jealousy are never attractive characters to display. We always work hard to hide or disguise it from friends and family members. It will come out in different ways, such as resentment and being highly critical and judgmental of others.

Competitiveness will dominate our relationships as we strive to be the top dog in the relationship. Becoming depressed and highly critical because we have not achieved what we desire and what others have will distract us and rob us of us. Scripture teaches us in John 10:10, "The thief comes to steal and kill and destroy, I have come that they may have life, and have it to the fullest."

The next level of the battle plan is disillusionment, that feeling of being lied to and that the game of life has been fixed against you from the beginning and no matter what you do, you'll never achieve your desired outcome. Many minority groups in America feel like this on a daily basis and are more susceptible to a "dysthymic disorder," which is a chronic low-grade depression. This disillusionment can be destructive in a person's life, for it can lead to a loss of hope and an attitude of giving up on life, which includes decreased energy, fluctuating body weight, depleted concentration, irritability, bouts of crying, hopelessness/despair, a disinterest in pleasurable activities, social withdrawal, and thoughts of suicide. The Bible is replete with examples of depression with a variety of reasons and results. King David wrote of his depression caused by unconfessed sin in Psalm 38:51. God used depression to get Nehemiah's attention in Nehemiah 1–2. Job's devastating losses led him to curse the day he was born (Job 1–3). And Elijah was so depressed over the situation with Israel's leaders that he wished to die (1 Kings 19).

The final attack of this unholy trinity is discouragement, which is a feeling of despair, sadness, lack of confidence, and feeling disheartened. Three connections contribute and bring this plan full circle:

- Lack of confidence in self
- Lack of confidence in God
- Lack of hope for the future

Because discouragement is a feeling or emotion, it can play games with our minds. We must learn how to control our minds, and thus discouragement, and lean on God for strength. Joshua was challenged with discouragement as he led the people of Israel into the Promised Land. God told Joshua, "Be strong and of good courage" (Joshua 1:6). God also reminded Joshua that the key to overcoming discouragement was a personal relationship with Him. The Lord told Joshua: "This Book of the Law shall not depart from your mouth, but you shall meditate in it day and night, that you may observe to do according to all that is written in it. For then you will make your way prosperous, and have good success" (Joshua 1:8). Discouraged people often blame themselves or God and ask, "What if . . .?" This is Satan's trap, his way of trying to have us think, "I blew it" or "God isn't capable." God has a much bigger picture for our lives than we could ever imagine. Challenges along the way are God's way of refining us, preparing us for the bigger and better picture. If not dealt with, discouragement can lead to depression that can stop people in their tracks. Discouragement reveals an unwillingness to trust God. It can be dealt a death blow when people consistently cast all their cares on God.

The Prize: Our Call, Our Purpose, Our Destiny

The million-dollar question that is always asked of God, and in some cases rhetorically, is "Why?" or better yet, "Why me?" This is an essential error in human thinking because we have the uncanny ability to make everything about us because our feelings are hurt and we are disappointed with God and life. But the reality of our internal torment goes far beyond envious and jealous people and far beyond the daily attacks we endure. Our problem is found in the Holy Scripture in John 3:16: "For God so loved the world that He gave His only begotten Son, that whoever believes in Him should not perish but have everlasting life." This eternal promise toward humanity has provoked a cosmic war, provoking an eternal evil adversary named Lucifer who was transformed to Satan.

Let us explore this for a few minutes. Shortly after Lucifer along with one-third of the angelic hosts were kicked out of heaven because of rebellion, something unusual took place at that moment. Their expulsion from heaven simply means a harsh rejection from God due to their arrogance and pride. Since they were rejected by God, their holiness, perfection, and goodness could not be sustained and maintained any longer.[20] They all have undergone a strange transformation that had never occurred prior to that. They were all transformed into evil spirits. Lucifer became Satan, and his legions of angels became demons.

In other contexts, "Satan" is a broad term used to describe an all-evil being. The term *Satan* means adversary—in other words, the one who is always there to oppose God and His people. Notably, there is no restoration for him. That's what draws a clear distinction between the fall of Lucifer and his legions of angels and the fall of humankind. The bottom line is, God has done something that truly transcended the history of humanity on behalf of all of us that He hasn't done for the fallen angels. God already had a plan to bring humanity back to Him through Christ before they even fell into sin. That plan was a mystery for Satan. This simply means that as long as we're alive,

---

20 https://www.living-for-jesus-alone.org. Why Satan Hates Humanity. Sept. 2014.

we're in an infinitely better position than Satan because we still have the oppor- tunity to be saved and inherit eternal life through Jesus alone.[21] Since the devil has a hold on every individual who is not yet saved, they are left with the responsibility to choose whom they are willing to serve.

So, the question still remains: why does Satan hate humanity to its core? First of all, when thinking about Satan's attitude toward mankind, one thing that we might say to ourselves is humanity didn't cause Satan to lose his position in heaven. Therefore, why go after humanity in such a wrathful manner? The main reason is Satan has found himself in a highly desperate situation, and he is trapped between both his past and his future. He cannot go back and take full responsibility for his rebellion in order for him to be restored by God. At the same time, there is a horrible, inescapable judg- ment pronounced against him that will eventually take

---

21 Ibid

place at some point during his existence. He is well aware of the fact that there is no restoration for him, and his time is running short. Revelation 12:12 says, "Therefore rejoice, O heavens, and you who dwell in them! Woe to the inhabitants of the earth and the sea! For the devil has come down to you, having great wrath, because he knows that he has a short time." Since he can't go back to heaven to take revenge against God Almighty who kicked him out of heaven, Satan, in his arrogance, pride, and full hatred toward God, wants to unleash his evil sentiments toward someone. As a result, he has embraced an approach to bring destruction to anything deemed valuable to God. Bear in mind, Satan's initial plan was to supersede God, and his desire to do so far excelled his very being as just a created being. We can conclude Satan harbors a hatred toward God, along with humanity that far exceeds his own nature. That hatred is the key factor that motivates him daily in his quest to further corrupt and destroy humanity. He's obsessed with doing so; his only weapons are sin and our weakness to it.[22]

We have been made in the very image of God. Genesis 1:26 says: "Then God said, 'Let Us make man in Our image, according to Our likeness; let them have dominion over the fish of the sea, over the birds of the air, and over the cattle, over all the earth and over every creeping thing that creeps on the earth.'" This design of humanity demonstrates we're important and special to God. However, it's not something that can be taken for granted because our significance only relies on our Maker. That is because if we're detached from God who is the source of our life and because of sin, that significance we possess doesn't matter.

There are several reasons as to why Satan hates us. The first reason is we're made in the image of God Almighty. The second is God has granted us an unmerited privilege that the enemy doesn't have. We have such a mind-blowing opportunity to go to heaven and

____

22 Ibid.

be with our Maker forever through Christ by escaping his control. That's truly what has intensified that hatred even further. Because Satan has been to heaven and knows the extraordinary beauty of the place, he doesn't want anybody to inherit what he has lost. This hatred attacks our call from God's purpose and final destiny.

Satan is a masterful influencer to the immature mind. He blinds people's eyes and minds so they cannot see the light of the gospel that displays the glory of Christ who is the image of God. He blinds people's minds toward the truth through immoral living and false beliefs. He influences people to rebel against God. Moreover, he influences people to believe they should have freedom for the sole purpose of doing whatever they want. He manipulates people into believing they can live their lives however they like without giving them time to think about the consequences of their sinful lifestyles. He imprints that deceptive belief in people's minds that the Word of God is all about keeping them from having fun, and the Word of God is all about men trying to control other people's lives. He holds them captive in sinful living. He influences people to become negligent and ignorant about their own eternity in the sense of being unwilling to accept Christ as their personal Savior. He truly is deception personified. These deceptions have the ability to make people walk away from their call, forfeit their purpose, and switch their destiny before they even know what they have done.

CHAPTER 6

TRAPPED BY THE MASK

Matthew 23:16 "Woe to you, blind guides, who say, 'Whoever swears by the temple, it is nothing; but whoever swears by the gold of the temple, he is obliged to perform it.' Fools and blind! For which is greater, the gold or the temple that sanctifies the gold?"

Pride and Arrogance

Pride

Many people over-imprison themselves in every aspect of life by their own pride and arrogance. The suitor who presents him or herself to be more than they are to win the affections of their heart's desire then has to keep up the charade. The employee who embellishes their pedigree and accomplishment to get the promotion but finds themselves over their heads when it's time to do the work. The politician who promises everything but can't deliver on those promises. The pastor who uses religion for personal gain while presenting oneself in a pious manner. Yes, many people entrap themselves into lives of emotional and spiritual bondage because of pride and arrogance. The flirtatious and adulterous wife who presents a happy home, full of love and affection, but can't resist any opportunity to flirt with male co-workers.

Pride and arrogance tend to alter character and

control temperament while creating falsehoods in our speech. Pride is a subtle but extremely dangerous sin; it's called the sin of sins. It was pride that got Lucifer tossed out of heaven and transformed. As Ezekiel 28:12 says, "Son of man, take up a lament concerning the king of Tyre and say to him, 'This is what the sovereign Lord says, "You were the seal of perfection, full of wisdom and perfect in beauty."'" It was the sin that misled Eve to eat the forbidden fruit and endure the judgment of a holy God. Pride is the foundation of all sin as it is the original sin that brought judgment on Satan, for out of pride comes all kinds of malice in the forms of envy, jealousy, resentment, anger, bitterness, and so on.

Let us take a moment to dig into this original sin called pride. When King Solomon said in Ecclesiastes "vanity of vanities" to describe what consumes human behavior in all aspects of human life, he was talking about the excessive pride we have in ourselves, our appearances, qualities, achievements, acquisitions, and even our access to rich, popular, or beautiful people.

The king even accused himself of the sin of pride in his lifelong pursuit for wisdom and knowledge. The sin of pride sets the trap for enslavement, whereas arrogance is the jailer who turns the key to the cell door. This is such an evil and rebellious characteristic that it singlehandedly can overpower the whole personality. It produces characteristically offensive behaviors of privilege, entitlement, disrespect, conceit, and disillusionment. Pride keeps us from calling on and submitting to God. It blinds us from our own sin by presenting our sin as commendable. It affects our eyesight, causing us to view ourselves through distorted lenses of reality. Our stubborn attitudes make us refuse to be kind so our attempt at reconciliation with people will be viewed as integrity, dignity, and "no longer a slave."

Yet, just as we easily filter out our own evil, we quickly filter in others and *find faults* all the time. The prideful have *harsh spirits* and display contempt, irritation, frustration, and judgment of others' sin. You will find pride in their dismissiveness toward others' struggles, in their sarcastic statements about their spouses, and even in their prayers. Prideful people are *superficial,* for they are more concerned with others' perceptions of them than the reality of their hearts. They fight the sins that impact how others see them while making peace with the sins no one sees. Pride make us *defensive* where we lack the ability to stand in the strength of imputed righteousness and resist verbal attacks from man and Satan. Humility is lost and replaced by the need to challenge or rebuke. Pride makes us presume and become *presumptuous* before God, placing demands, conditions, and ultimatums on Him. Pride makes us crave attention and have insatiable appetites for respect and worship. Some boast, some are never satisfied, and some are haunted by hidden desires. Prideful people are often neglectful of others; they tend to value some people over others, and they tend to honor those who the world deems worthy of honor, giving more weight to their words, their wants, and their needs. Prideful people get a thrill when people of power and significance acknowledge them.

Arrogance

Arrogance is best described as a haughty person who acts as if they are superior and more valuable or important than others and underestimates them. Arrogance implies a desire to dominate and excessive confidence in one's abilities, as well as seeing oneself as worthy of success. This mask of pride and arrogance that we put on deeply affects the pathology of our thinking that we, the wearers of these masks, begin to believe our own hypocrisy. The danger of this dynamic is we have no problem vaunting and flaunting our pride and arrogance against God and in some cases use His holy Word to support this behavior. However, a holy God will always humble the proud as he did with Peninnah, Eli's sons, the Philistines, Goliath, Saul, Nabal, Absalom, Shimei, Sheba, and even King David.

These toxic twins have even made God's top six list in Proverbs 6:16–17: "These six things the Lord hates, yes seven are an abomination to Him: A proud look." As you can see, it's the first one of the seven detestable sins that provides a glimpse into the sinfulness of man, beginning with the mask of pride and arrogance, for as pride is the sin, and arrogance is the manifested performance and characteristics of our pride. This sin blinds us from a foundational truth about ourselves and our relationships with God first and people second. Our relationship with God is based on His desire to be in relationship with us because of His love and deep concern for the utterly lost who were born in sin and shaped in iniquity. Our part of this relationship is thankfulness, humility, and submission to His will. Our relationship with each other should always be built on servanthood. Pride and arrogance destroy these relationships. With God, there is no submission because the prideful believe in their hearts that their success is by their hand, and their failure is by others' schemes against them, and God is there to present the proud righteousness and acceptance to all. We are front-row witnesses to the destructiveness of this narcissistic ideology in our society today, where the polarization among nations, races, politics, and regions of our country, friends, couples, and spouses is frightening. Everyone wants to be right, heard, and seen, so we weaponize victimization and deliver strikes through social media outlets where encouragement and support for destruction is easily found. Beloved, as long as this internal hidden war stays locked away in your mind and heart, you will continue to struggle between blessings and curses, positivity and negativity, joy and pain with no consistency continuing to be tossed to and fro by false prophets, false friends, and hypocrites.

Hypocrisy and Hype

In this internal campaign of aggression for control of our minds, beliefs, and behaviors, pride and arrogance are covert but deadly agents that, if successful in getting to our hearts and minds, can relegate our testimonies, speech, and witnessing to hypocrisy and hype. Romans 12:3 says, "For I say, through the grace given unto me, to every man that is among you, not to think of himself more highly than he ought to think; but to think soberly, according as God hath dealt to every man the measure of faith." The warning from the apostle here is simple: "see yourself in the framework of a much bigger picture." As you and I have achieved according to the measure of faith given unto us, so have others also achieved and accomplished according to theirs. It is our duty to give God all the glory for our achievements, allow His increase in all of me as I decrease. Yet, pride and arrogance perverts the process and internally switches the motivation to hypocrisy and hype.

If God is God all by Himself and does not need any of us to promote His will, then why ask us to? Salvation is free, but deliverance costs, and all of us have to lose some things and give up old desires of the flesh for new and better ones of the spirit. And it looks like this: my joy and happiness of my achievements should not be in the achievement, work, or struggle to achieve, but rather in the opportunity given that allowed me to achieve. The difference here is our testimony should not be based on a human and or material plateaus reached, but rather consistently on the God whose goodness is the same yesterday, today, and forevermore. If the testimony and praise report is based on what you and I have been allowed to achieve, we now sub- consciously make it about us and not all about God. Isaiah 42:8 says, "I am the Lord: that is my name: and my glory will I not give to another, neither my praise to graven images." This is the problem with the church today. Instead of pointing the lost to Jesus Christ, the author and finisher of our faith, we try to draw and attract men and women through the prism of attraction, sensationalism, and the promise that belonging to this church or that church will increase your faith, improve your life, and attain a measure of prosperity.

Now our denominational doctrine of inclusion has become sectarian and exclusive in that one's ministry has the best understanding, pontificates the deepness of the gospel, and gets you closer to God. What an arrogant, prideful, and detestable presentation of God's holy church that traps all in a downward spiral of hypocrisy and hype. And the evidence is clear: a conservative estimate is that attendance is down in the Western church some forty percent, while in Asia, India, and Africa, Christianity in the last century in Africa is up from ten million in 1900 to the year 2000 when four hundred million people identify themselves as Christians. The Western crusades worked better on good and humble soil in foreign lands than in our own land. Conservatively speaking, about fifty percent or more people who identify themselves as Christians don't attend church services regularly and if they do, won't give a testimony. But they will not have a problem testifying among friends and on social media about how good God has been to them because of what they now have or achieved—meaning their status and possessions. In other words, they prefer the God of this world that allows them to become the center of their own world rather than letting the God of Abraham, Isaac, and Jacob be the center of their life, and everything else must revolve around Him that comes into our lives.

This dangerous self-worship ideology is rooted deeply in idolatry, for it is nothing more than a self-focused, self-absorbed psychological session with one goal and aim in mind—to make us feel good about ourselves for a time. Because these sessions are limited, the feel-good euphoria is not long lasting and needs to be reignited and reenergized. The reason why salvation is so elusive to the Western church and why those in it don't see the relevance of the church in their lives is because of self-worship this society of saints believes: "They must be satisfied rather than God glorified in their worship, then we put God below ourselves as though he had been made for us rather than that we had been made for Him" (Stephen Charnock). The First and Second Commandments are:

- Thou shalt have no other gods before me.
- Thou shalt not make unto thee any graven image, or any likeness of anything.

Our insatiable desire to be evaluated and approved by people and God, based on status, wealth, accomplishments, and possessions, is a tragic violation of these two commandments. And because we have created and live in a consumeristic society and world, it can be difficult to see who God is. This is why most Christians today practice a schizophrenic type of Christianity in that they quote much scripture, but live and or believe none of it.

Schizophrenic Saints

We all were, at one time or another, one of these saints in our Christian walk, so I don't write this section to ridicule, condemn, or criticize, but rather to help recognize. The apostle Paul wrote these words in 1 Corinthians 13:11, "When I was a child, I spoke as a child, I understood as a child, I thought as a child: but when I became a man, I put away childish things." It is not my intention to minimize those who suffer with this devastating psychosis of the mind. My only point here is to show the deep inconsistencies between beliefs and behaviors. In my first book, *The Corporate Christian: Christian Beliefs vs. Corporate Behaviors*, I talked about this dynamic from the point of view of identifying the tenets of each doctrine, Christianity and corporations, where they are compatible and where they are at odds, and how the corporate saint must be contented in boundaries of their behavioral limits. Here, I am describing that saint, whether they be in any environment, the inconsistency of temperament and behavior, based on how said environments affect their emotional stability, which affects professional coping, marital relationships, self-esteem, and many of the forty most common other disorders the Diagnostic and Statistical Manual of Mental Disorders (DSMV) says affect most people at one time or another.

In spite of our unwillingness to submit and obey, God still holds out for us the one basic solution to peaceful and productive daily living. 2 Timothy 1:7 says, "For God has not given us a spirit of fear, but of power and of love and of a sound mind," that is the power to overcome fear and anx- iety, bitterness and resentment, discouragement and depression, and to stabilize our temperament and fulfill our contentment without having to show or prove to ourselves if we are right with Him. As the tagline scripture to begin this chapter states: "Fools and blind! For which is greater, the gold, or the temple that sanctifies it."

CHAPTER 7

THE BATTLE OVER OUR IDOLS

Romans 1:22–23 "Professing themselves to be wise, they became fools, and changed the glory of the uncorruptible God into an image made like to corruptible man, and to birds, and four-footed beasts, and creeping things."

I dolatry worship was a never-ending problem for biblical and ancient man, as it is today. Idolatry is worshipping other things besides the one true God. Consistently, throughout the Bible, it is made clear that idolatry is unacceptable. In the times of the Bible, most people worshipped gods and goddesses made of stone, wood, or sometimes precious metals. God condemns the worship of such objects. No matter what the idol is made of, it is still a lifeless object with no power or character. It definitely has no power to save us from our sins! Idolatry is not only foolish but is a major sin in the eyes of God.

As time has passed and man evolved in knowledge, skills, exploration, and destructive power, his idolatry has become bolder and more blatant. And the battle to overcome his idolatry is nonexistent. Idolatry is another weapon of Satan's, meant for us as God's creation, to deny Him as we live and enjoy the wonders and majesties of His creation. Satan is truly the most cunning beast in the garden, as he perverts the ethos of the things

God has given us for good, to mature and grow us to be able to receive the best He has in store for us.[23] At its core, idolatry is rooted in childish selfishness and is amplified to the tenth power when we become adults. The selfish need to feel better than others can drive some to live partial lives around what they desire, and these desires or idols spark a psychological reaction of pride in oneself, based on feeling superior, better, and greater than most others. Satan will use our own lives, achievements, and accomplishments as evidence why we idolize self or our education, job, career, wealth, home/property, cars, lifestyle, and status.

This process in winning the battle of the hidden war when we believe all of the above has been ordained by Christ for you because you prayed, sacrificed, gave, or did some extraordinary feat in Christendom for many Christians is first to recognize that they have placed idols before our Holy God. They have been duped by

---

23 Dana, Carson. *One True King* (Dana Carson Ministries, 2010), 34.

the father of lies, but they weren't the first and certainly won't be the last.

During the prophet Micah's time, the people of Israel were also duped into idolatry. It was a time of prosperity in the land, and the elite became rich; their behavior reflected their newfound riches and wealth. They lost forgiveness in their hearts for their neighbors, servants, and slaves. They indulged in lifestyles not representative of covenant living. Yet, on the Sabbath, they would come down with great big offerings to the temple. These offerings made them feel spiritually and psychologically good within themselves. Because of their idolatry and how good it felt, they never knew God and performed public acts of piety before Him. So, God brought a charge against them and their characters with judgment to follow. He concluded, through the prophet, what we already know He requires from us in Micah 6:8, "He has shown you, O man, what is good; And what the Lord requires of you but to do justly, to love mercy, and to walk humbly with your God."

The key to winning this battle will lie in your ability to recognize and destroy Satan's perversion of God's provisions in our lives. If we don't give into the allure of making our idols our gods because of how they make us feel, we begin to sever deep-rooted affections for objects that give us psychological, emotional, and spiritual highs while at the same time are leading our eternal souls into damnation, killing our influence with people, and presenting us as shallow, condescending, social climbers.

Dr. Dana Carson in his book, *One True King*, identifies idols as anything that gets in the way of our putting God first in our lives always. He goes on to identify a few of these modern-day idols. (I say "modern-day idols" because most of us are no longer building pyramids, statues of animals, or celestial bodies.) But we do make idols of family, career, wealth, and "isms."

Over the years, as a pastor and counselor, I have noticed idol worshipping is not a random supernatural event where we, the Christian, are helpless, but rather, how we worship and what we worship seem to connect with our characteristics and/or nature. So, the battle must be fought in our personalities, which is the most difficult type of disorder to overcome.

- Narcissists may be comfortable with worshipping a successful career.
- Controllers may be comfortable with worshipping family.
- Lovers of money may be comfortable with worshipping wealth.
- Narcissists, hateful and insecure people, and those with low self-esteemed may be comfortable with racism, sexism, and denominationalism.

It was said to me once by one of my counselee's: "Water seeks its own level," meaning people are more comfortable with behaviors and environments familiar to them.

Narcissism and Careers

The word *narcissism* originates from Greek mythology about Narcissus. According to the myth, he was a man who *sees his own reflection in a pool of water and falls in love with it.* Having an over- the-top sense of one's physical perfection is certainly a foundational characteristic of narcissistic personality disorder (NPD). This disorder encompasses three essential features: (1) An exaggerated sense of self-importance, (2) a preoccupation with being admired, and (3) poor ability to empathize with or take the perspective of others. The narcissist is so self-absorbed and preoccupied with garnering admirations from others that he or she can be an extremely unpleasant person to work with, let alone have a relationship with.[24]

Based in fear, deep insecurities and vulnerabilities are masked with exaggerated amounts of self-confidence.

---

24 W. Brad Johnson, William. L Johnson. *The Minister's Guide to Psychological Disorders and Treatments* (Routledge, 2014), 1.

To keep up the performance, the narcissist makes themselves the center of their world, and everyone around them will comply. They lack empathy for anyone and will turn all conversations back to them. There are two types of narcissists: the grandiose narcissist and the vulnerable narcissist. Both share the same features but are not the same. They overlap with shared feelings of entitlement, have a proclivity toward antagonism, and use manipulation when power, control, and self-esteem are being threatened. Grandiose narcissists have an overabundance of high self-esteem while vulnerable narcissists operate on extremely low self-esteem. But their mission and goal are the same: to use things like career to satisfy their sense of superiority and entitlement among us commoners. This personality disorder seeks to use the idol of career to evict God out of the person's heart.

Controller and Family

Controlling disorders are better known as "borderline

personality disorders." At its core, this behavior seeks compliance to its needs, wants, and desires. These individuals may seem like they are choosing family first and then God, but in reality, may well be suffering from fear of abandonment issues. These types of people need constant reassurance that the family relationship/unit is intact. Even if the relationship has become unstable by their own hand, they tend to exist between idealizing and devaluing their relationships and splitting it into a love and hate one.

Greed and Wealth

Greed is the one thing that connects all addiction. A rich and popular person was once asked the question, "How much is enough?" His answer was, "A little bit more." As addicts progress (or rather, regress) into their addiction, to derive sufficient gratification, they must constantly seek more and more of their drug of choice, for *more* is the keyword of addiction. It doesn't matter whether they're addicted to a substance, relationship, or activity, the "ante" for getting enough of the object of their craving must continually be raised.

Of all the things one might be addicted to, nothing tops the greed-laden pursuit of wealth in its audacity, manipulativeness, and gross insensitivity to the needs and feelings of others, not to mention its extreme, short-sighted, irresponsible covetousness. Ask a multimillionaire or billionaire so afflicted (if you can find one willing to talk to you), and you'll discover their "mega-fortune quest" has no end point. They won't be able to name the definitive "millionth" or "billionth" that will finally do it for them. They can't because the means by which they reap their riches has itself become the end.[25]

Narcissist and "-isms"

Narcissism is not only about hiding low self-esteem issues through grandiose or vulnerable behavioral pathologies.

---

25 Leon F Seltzer, Evolution of Self, *Psychology Today*, October 17, 2012.

There is also a real dark side to this disorder. Narcissists can attack in many antisocial and volatile ways when they feel threatened or are denied the attention they seek and crave. They can be disingenuous, disrespectful, manipulative, slanderous, opinionated, argumentative, lack empathy, cause division, hypocritical, and more. This is why -isms fit in so well with this disorder.

FIGHTING IN THE LIGHT

John 1:4–5 "In Him was life, and the life was the light of men. And the light shines in the darkness, and the darkness did not comprehend it."

What or Who Is the Light?

The Holy Writ is clearly talking about what and who it's describing in these two verses. To get more support, the first three verses go back to the beginning and introduce us to the pre-incarnate work of Jesus Christ. The apostle John bridges the gap between the power of the living Word and Christ and His illuminating attribute. So, fighting in the light is simply fighting in the security of Christ. The gospel message, which is the living Word, has the power to bring forth a new life out of an old one. The catalyst for this process is the illuminating power of the light. But let us not be fooled—this only works if one is truly honest with oneself with a mature desire to not just do better but be better.

Some earlier theological interpretations suggest the word *comprehend* should be *apprehend*, meaning any encounter with Christ will bring about life transformation in all facets of a person's life. Fighting in the light is a home field advantage for the Christian, yet many of us feel like it's a handicap because we can't express our naturally angry, volatile temperament.

Yet, the reality here is, in the light, you are not the one fighting at all. When we submit and are apprehended by the light, we come into the presence of God's character and attributes.

Apprehension and Comprehension of the Light

One of the elders in the church where I have pastored for the last seventeen years talks about this process using the "Fruit of the Spirit" story. The Spirit of God interacts with us through nine characteristics that capture and transform us: *love, joy, peace, long-suffering, kindness, goodness, faithfulness, gentleness,* and *self-control.* These nine personality traits don't operate independently of each other but feed and grow from each other, starting with the main foundation—love. Love is a dominant character trait of the Godhead, for by it, men have been eternally saved. We learn to suffer for it, submit because of it, and grow through it. When love gets through with us, we have such internal joy and peace knowing we have done what is right in all things, no matter if the outcome was in our favor or not.

Love, joy, and peace move us into contentment with ourselves and others, knowing our life is pleasing to God. When a person is content, they are more willing to be patient and kind and perform good deeds to and for others. When Christ has developed us spiritually, it's easier for us to develop better external relationships as well as our personal development in areas of being more faithful, gentle, and exercising better self-control in our relationships with Christ and others.

Hosea 4:6 says, "My people are destroyed for lack of knowledge. Because you have rejected knowledge, I also will reject you from being priest for me; because you have forgotten the law of your God, I also will forget your children."

When Christians decide to reject knowledge because of arrogance, pride, and love for the things in the world, they have put themselves on a path toward destruction. They have chosen to fight on foreign soil and have lost the home field advantage. In Psalm 1, David says the man who refuses to walk by the counsel of the ungodly, stand with sinners, not befriend the scornful, but instead seeks and learns the law of the Lord will be like a tree planted by the rivers of water. I personally love this analogy, as one who has, over the last thirty-five years of life, certainly learned the meaning of being connected to Christ as well as not being connected to Him. As trees are planted in the ground, their roots develop much faster than the exposed tree. The roots grow strong and thick as they spread deep into the earth, looking to cover as much ground as possible to find water and absorb as much rainfall as possible. This water nourishes the tree as sap, which enables the tree to have strong trunks and branches. So, if we the vines and leaves are connected to the strong branches, we now look like and represent the tree to which we are connected.

Representation demands compliance, and compliance demands knowledge. As long as we stay connected, we are in the knowledge of the light, the power of the light, the comfort of the light, and the liberty and contentment of the light.

Power Attributes of the Light

God has many attributes—as a matter of fact, an entire graduate program can be taught on the attributes of God alone. But for this section, I will discuss the power of the light. Scripture teaches God is all-powerful, present, and knowing, but those aren't attributes that we as fallen people can attain. So, let's look toward the light, Jesus Christ, and emulate a few of His attributes in our lives.

Compassion

Jesus never looked away from people; He always looked upon them and had compassion. Matthew 9:36 says, "But when He saw the multitudes, He was moved with compassion for them, because they were weary and scattered, like sheep having no shepherd." Whenever people were around Him, Jesus understood their real needs and sought to address them. For some, physical healing was necessary; for others, the root issue was spiritual. In all cases though, Jesus took the time to notice people were hurting, and His compassion drove Him to help them.

Servanthood

Without a doubt, Jesus was the ultimate servant. Although He was praised as a great teacher and even had a decent following, He made sure to teach His followers to be servants by doing it Himself. In Mark 10:45, Jesus even tells everyone: "the Son of Man came not to be served but to serve." Despite having the authority to get anything He wanted and have people praise and pamper Him, He did the exact opposite by lowering Himself and serving others.

Love

Obviously, Jesus had a love for others. If He didn't, He wouldn't be compassionate nor a servant. Jesus claimed there is no greater love than to die for one of your friends, and He did just that. John 15:13 says, "Greater love has no one than this, than to lay down one's life for his friends." If anyone doubts His love, all they have to do is look upon the cross and see the agony that He bore for their sakes. He experienced that horrible death so that all can be saved. That clearly is true love at its finest.

Forgiveness

One of the most startling things said in Scripture is found in Luke 23:34, when Jesus is on the cross and proclaims: "Father, forgive them, for they know not what they do." Even while bleeding and experiencing pain, Jesus had His heart set on forgiveness—even forgiving those who put Him there in the first place! This is contrary to the everyday mantra of looking out for number one and obtaining personal justice. Jesus was by no means concerned for His own life; all He wanted was to provide a way for forgiveness.

These attributes are the power source of the light and the only reason why we need to stay here. Not only will it guarantee us current and eternal victory but also give us an understanding of life that we never knew because of the blindfolds of self-absorption.

CHAPTER 9

THE PEACE WE SEEK

John 14:27 "Peace I leave with you, my peace I give to you; not as the world gives do, I give to you. Let not your heart be troubled, neither let it be afraid."

Our Peace versus God's Peace

The one commodity modern-day man can't buy, trade, or negotiate for is peace. Inner peace, or peace within, is peace of mind and contentment. Wall Street does not trade it, and Walmart doesn't carry it on its shelves. There are many formulas and methodologies to attaining peace; a lot of them have to do with finding a quiet place, meditation, and or freeing oneself of worldly possessions. These do work for some, but how and where can you find peace when you are or, more specifically, your character is your tormentor? How can you free yourself from your own ambitions, your own ethical standards, and your own belief systems? The opposite of peace is war or chaos. These dynamics tend to raise stress levels, heighten senses, and put the mental and physical body on alert. What can stem the tide of worry, fear, anger, and disappointment in our hearts when the unpredictability of life's circumstances visits our homes, jobs, children, or parents? What blocks the fulfillment of ambition, frightens us into compromising standards, and brings into question belief systems about God and His provision, protection, and delivering power in our lives when the bottom looks like it has fallen out?

Peace can feel like an elusive concept in our global society today, so most settle for surface peace—peace in the moment, which erroneously means peace when happy with good friends, when hanging out at a nice restaurant, or when a demanding boss leaves us alone. Sadly, we attach conditions to our peace and limit peace to the distracting or entertaining of our hearts. This always makes man's peace fleeting and empty. The Christian who lives in fear of the world, judges the world, and looks down on the unsaved and unchurched, they don't have peace, for they are operating in a manner that is not conducive to peace. Peace is a gift from Christ to us; it protects our heart from being troubled and disturbed; it brings calm and confidence to people in times when they should be anxious, stressed, and consumed with worry. This kind of peace surpasses all human understanding. It's designed to protect, not entertain, limiting God's ability to give you His gift of peace by attaching conditions to it, which is a common mistake we all make. Peace is not the byproduct of the blessing of a new job because it stopped the torment of the old one. It's not the byproduct of human achievements or accomplishments because these things bring about status, respect among peers, and prestige. Peace is all about contentment.

The Real Enemy of Peace

The enemy to our peace is not always the opposite of our peace. Over many years of counseling people in general and in my own life struggles, I've found our peace is disturbed by the simplest things. It's not the size of a storm, but rather anticipating the arrival of it. In other words, our biggest enemy to our peace is our lack of faith and the instability of our minds in these moments.

Isaiah 59:19 says, "So they shall fear the name of

the Lord from the west, and His glory from the rising of the sun; when the enemy comes in like a flood, The Spirit of the Lord will lift up a standard against him." In this scripture from the prophet Isaiah, we see the totality of this hidden war—the surprise attack against our person, designed to frighten, paralyze, and confuse the mind so the imparted word/standard is lost in a moment of panic. Peace is gone, faith is gone, and instability is the thought for the day.

Instability represents doubt, uneasiness, and double mindedness. These are terrible characteristics to lean on in time of battle because they manipulate emotions, betray perception, and delude vision. When this happens, we are like a ship in a storm without a rudder. We are at the mercy of the destructive winds and crashing waves. This raging storm, blowing in your emotions, thoughts, and feelings will look something like this. We become emotionally spent due to the bipolar effect on us. We will flow between tears, sadness, anger, and cursing. As previously mentioned, our confidence in making sound decisions could be hampered by anger, fear, and depression. We may temporarily lose our love and joy in the trauma of the attack. If not managed properly, it can linger in our hearts for a lifetime. This last lingering phase is critical because it can change our character drastically. It opens the door for another enemy to our peace, and that's the blame game where we attach our storms to a particular person, place, or thing, which leads us into the disorder of bitterness.

Bitterness is to be avoided at all costs. It is an attitude of extended and intense anger and hostility. It is often accompanied by resentment and a desire to get even. It is a result of not forgiving an offender and letting the hurt and anger grow until resentment sours the person's view of life. It is also a sin that destroys life. Hebrews 12:14-15 says, "Make every effort to live in peace with everyone and to be holy; without holiness no one will see the Lord. See to it that no one falls short of the grace of God and that no bitter root grows up to cause trouble and defile many." This scripture warns bitterness corrupts with its poison. Romans 12:17–19 commands us not to seek revenge, but let God avenge the wrong: "Do not repay anyone evil for evil. Be careful to do what is right in the eyes of everyone. If it is possible, as far as it depends on you, live at peace with everyone."

Everlasting Peace

The concept of everlasting peace is not one that is common to humanity, nor is it a realistic goal to strive for while living in the physical flesh. But it is a central goal of the Christian faith. Revelation 21:4–6 says:

And God will wipe away every tear from their eyes; there shall be no more death, nor sorrow, nor crying. There shall be no more pain, for the former things have passed away." Then He who sat on the throne said, "Behold, I make all things new." And He said to me, "Write, for these words are true and faithful." And He said to me, "it is done! I am the Alpha and the

Omega, the Beginning and the End. I will give of the fountain of the water of life freely to him who thirsts."

All believers are motivated by living the life set forth by Christ with full assurance that if they keep the faith, fight the good fight, and finish their race, Revelation 21:4-6 will be their reality. It's a belief system that transforms lives, makes us endure calamity, hardship, unfairness, and in the timeless words of Job, "Yea He slay me, I will still trust Him." This promise is all most need to win the hidden wars in their lives, reconcile relationships, become more generous with their finances, and yes, change from selfish youths to selfless adults.

So, as you continue to grow in faith and walk in love, also remember the words of the apostle Paul in Ephesians 5:15, "See that you walk circumspectly, not as fools but as wise, redeeming the time, because the days are evil."

BIBLIOGRAPHY

Carson, Dana. One True King. Dana Carson Ministries, 2010.

Carter, L. Stephen. *Civility Manners, Morals, and the Etiquette of Democracy*. Harper Perennial, 1998.

Clinton, Tim, Hawkins, Ron. *The Quick Reference Guide Biblical Counseling Personal and Emotional Issues*. Baker Books, 2009.

Enns, Paul. *The Moody Handbook of Theology*. Moody Publishers, 1989.

Entwistle, N. David. *Integrative Approaches to Psychology and Christianity*. Cascade Books 2015.

Falwell, Jerry. *Building Dynamic Faith*. Thomas Nelson, Inc, 2005.

Johnson, W. Brad, Johnson, L. Johnson. *The Minister's Guide to Psychological Disorders and Treatments*. Routledge Publishers, 2014.

Kollar, Allen. Charles. *Solution Focus Pastoral Counseling*. Zondervan, 1997.

Seltzer, F. Leon. Evolution of Self. *Psychology Today*, 2012.

MORE ABOUT PASTOR WILLIAMS

Pastor Owen E. Williams is the Pastor of the St. Mark Missionary Baptist church where he has served as senior pastor for the last Seventeen years. He is also the retired Director of Pastoral Care Services at the New York City Health and Hospitals Corporation Kings County Hospital. There, he oversaw the spiritual care for the seven-hundred-bed public hospital. Pastor Williams has a master's degree in Pastoral Counseling, an Honorary Doctorate in Divinity, and a bachelor's degree in Criminal Justice. He is the author of four published books, ***The Corporate Christian: Christian Beliefs Vs. Corporate Behaviors, The Corporate Christian 2: The Battle for your Beliefs, The Corporate Christian 3: The Hidden War***, and ***American Christianity: Black Liberation White Legalism*** the President of the Queens Federation of Churches Board of Directors, former NYPD clergy liaison for the 103rd Precinct, a former member of the Board of Directors for Live on NY, the second largest OPO (Organ Procurement Organization) in North America, and the founder and President of OE Williams Ministries.

Pastor Williams frequently travels to Johannesburg, South Africa, where he conducts training seminars on Solution Focus Pastoral Counseling for social workers, schoolteachers, police officers, and clergy.

Pastor Williams has been married to Elder Debora Williams, his wife for over 32 years, and they have one daughter, Desiree Rose Williams.

Throughout Pastor Williams' Christian journey, the

Lord has taught him many things, but two things have always stayed with him; maximize your moments, we have so few, and an ounce of practice is worth a ton of preaching.

Let us all be practitioners rather than preachers of the gospel, doers rather than hear of the word.

www.ingramcontent.com/pod-product-compliance
Lightning Source LLC
Chambersburg PA
CBHW021207130726
47988CB00002B/541